Are good marriages made in heaven?

It's true. God has brought you two together (for better or
for worse, for richer or for poorer...). But if you want to keep
heaven in your marriage, you've got to come down to earth.
As Ken Abraham says, "A good marriage takes work—lots
of work!"

In *Unmasking the Myths of Marriage*, you'll find out how to
give up the fantasies and myths you brought into your
marriage and happily trade them for the realities.

You won't find any "quick-fix solutions" — but you will
find practical suggestions to help you work at your marriage so your marriage will work for you. Throughout
these pages, Ken reminds you that when it comes to
dealing with marital mayhem, it helps to keep your sense
of humor!

Trade those starry eyes for eyes of wisdom and understanding. Read *Unmasking the Myths of Marriage*.

BY **Ken Abraham**
Don't Bite the Apple 'Til You Check for Worms
Designer Genes
Hot Trax (Devotions for Girls)
Hot Trax (Devotions for Guys)
Positive Holiness
Unmasking the Myths of Marriage

For information regarding
speaking engagements and seminars,
please write:

Ken Abraham
P.O. Box 218
Clymer, PA 15728

UNMASKING THE MYTHS OF MARRIAGE

KEN ABRAHAM

Power Books

Fleming H. Revell Company
Old Tappan, New Jersey

Library of Congress Cataloging–in–Publication Data

Abraham, Ken.
    Unmasking the myths of marriage / Ken Abraham.
      p. cm.
    ISBN 0-8007-5347-X
    1. Marriage—United States. 2. Marriage—Religious aspects —Christianity. I. Title.
HQ734.A187 1990   90-8130
306.81'0973—dc20   CIP

TO Angela, my wife,
who knows me at my best
and at my worst . . . and still loves me!

Contents

Contents

Contents

1
Things You Wish You Had Known Before You Married!

"Some marriages are made in heaven . . . but so are
thunder and lightning!"

● ● ● ● ● ● ● ● ● ● ● ● ● ● ●

The message light on our telephone-answering machine
was flashing furiously when my wife, Angela, and I
stepped through the doorway of our home.

"Either we got a lot of calls while we were gone or
somebody must really be trying to get in touch with us,"
I commented to Angela as I rewound the machine filled
with messages.

"Maybe there's an emergency at the church," Angela
suggested as she lugged a suitcase toward the bedroom.

"I'll soon find out." I pressed "play" and picked up a
pen and notepad to jot down the messages. I quickly realized, however, that nearly all of the messages on the
machine were from the same two people! And, yes, it was
an emergency . . . at least, it was to them.

"Pastor Ken!" the giddy voice on the tape impishly im-
plored. "This is Shelly. Barry and I need to talk to you
right away. Please call me at this number as soon as you
get home."

The next voice belonged to a male. "Hi, Ken. This is Barry. Would you *please* call either Shelly or me as soon as possible. It's an emergency. Well, it's not really an *emergency*," Barry laughed before continuing, "but it's an emergency to us."

The following message was from Shelly again. "Pastor Ken. Puh-leeze call me. We need you. Hurry!"

What in the world is going on here? I wondered as the tape continued to play. A few messages from individuals other than Shelly or Barry rolled by before the couple dominated my answering machine again.

This time both Shelly's and Barry's voices were on the tape. They were laughing hysterically. "Pastor Ken! Calling Pastor Ken. Wherever you are. Come in please, Pastor Ken. This is Barry . . . and this is Shelly . . . and we want to get married! This weekend! Call us, will you please?"

I stopped the tape and sat down. *Married? Why, they've only been dating for a couple of weeks! This weekend? They've got to be joking!*

I hastily dialed Barry's phone number.

No answer.

I tried Shelly. She responded on the first ring.

"Hello, Shelly? This is Ken Abraham."

"Oh! Pastor Ken! I'm so glad to hear from you. Barry and I thought that we were going to have to get married without you! I want you to marry me."

"Well, thank you, Shelly. I'm honored. But I'm already married, and I don't think Angela would appreciate that."

"Huh? Oh." Shelly laughed at my feeble joke. "No, you know what I mean—Barry and I want you to perform our wedding ceremony. This weekend."

"What are you talking about, Shelly? What's all this about getting married? And why the big rush?"

"That's right, Pastor Ken. Barry and I want to get married this weekend. We know we are right for each other. We love each other and we can't see any reason to wait any longer."

"But you've only been dating a few weeks," I protested.

"Two and a half weeks, to be exact," she chirped.

"Two and a half weeks? You hardly know each other!"

"Oh, no. Barry and I have been acquainted for years, but it's only been in the past two weeks that we've really gotten to *know* each other, if you know what I mean."

"No, I don't know what you mean. Have you and Barry been sleeping together?" I asked bluntly, fearing that their reason for wanting such a hasty wedding might be guilt over premarital sex, or worse, that Shelly might be pregnant.

"Oh, my, no!" Shelly answered, laughing. "But we'd sure like to—I can't say that we haven't been tempted."

I took a deep breath and let it out slowly. *Well, at least we don't have to deal with that problem . . . yet*, I thought.

I spoke sternly into the telephone. "Shelly. Listen to me. You and Barry both know my policy on weddings. I won't marry any couple who has not had a minimum of six one-hour counseling sessions, and normally, we spread those out over several months."

"Are you saying that you won't marry us?" Shelly asked, surprise in her voice.

"I'm saying that I won't marry you two *this weekend*. Besides, I'm going to be out of town this weekend and I won't be back for two more weeks. Why don't you and

13

Barry cool things down a bit and we'll get together to talk about this when I get back?"

I shook my head as I placed the phone back in its cradle and prayed, "Lord, help them."

Two weeks later, Angela and I returned from our trip, only to be met by another barrage of blinking lights and frantic messages on our answering machine.

"Pastor Ken! Please get back to me right away!" It was Barry.

"Hello? Pastor Ken. This is Shelly. Please call me right now. It's an emergency!" Then, as if she could read my mind, she added, "I mean it's *really* an emergency this time!"

Oh, no! What did she do? I wondered. I stopped the answering machine and dialed Shelly's number.

After six or seven rings, just as I was getting ready to hang up, I heard Shelly's voice. "Hello?" she said softly, as if she were being roused out of a deep sleep.

"Hello, Shelly. This is Ken Abraham. I just got home and found your message. What can I do for you?"

"Oh! Pastor Ken. Oh. Well, I just wanted to tell you that Barry and I got married two weeks ago, but it's not working, and we want a divorce."

"You what!" I nearly shouted into the phone's mouthpiece.

"Which one?" asked Shelly. "Why did we get married, or why do we want a divorce?"

"Both!" I bellowed. "Shelly! How could you do such a thing? Didn't I ask you to wait until I returned so we could talk about this?"

"Yes, but two weeks is such a long time when you're in love. After all, Barry and I are both in our thirties, and we've known each other for so long. We never dreamed that being married would change us so much, so quickly. We were great as friends but lousy as lovers. Now we realize we are almost totally incompatible!

"Maybe we were too starry-eyed, or perhaps we thought marriage was some sort of miracle drug that would magically transform the rest of our lives. Or maybe we simply believed too many myths about marriage before we plunged into it.

"Regardless, I wish we had known *then* what we know *now*."

● ● ● ● ● ● ● ● ● ● ● ● ● ● ●

Although you and your marriage partner may have been less impulsive than Shelly and Barry, perhaps their sentiments sound familiar to you. Don't you wish somebody could have warned you? Wouldn't it have been helpful if somebody, *anybody*—Mom, Dad, your pastor, Phil, Oprah, or Geraldo—had unmasked the myths about marriage and told you the messy truth?

You are not alone. Millions of marriage partners are sleeping in that same bed.

The Best-Kept Lies of Marriage

If you are like most people who get married, you expected your relationship to be great. Oh, sure, prior to your marriage, you heard the horror stories about some of your friends who had experienced marital troubles; a few got divorced before you decided to get married. But that was *them*. They must have done something wrong. Your marriage would be different.

Then the problems came. Pressures mounted. Stress

15

stretched every fiber of your being until, some days, you began to wonder, *Why bother?*

People who enter into marriage unprepared for handling adjustments, marital differences, problems, or disappointments sometimes panic when they discover their marriage isn't all they expected it to be. Some partners begin to doubt God's direction.

"Maybe we weren't really right for each other."

"Maybe we made a big mistake."

"Maybe we should bail out before things get any worse!"

Satan often adds to these misgivings by subtly suggesting, "You *had* the right person to marry, but you let that one slip away!"

Don't be deceived. Two factors separate those couples who choose to stay together from those who split up after a short stab at marriage. First, those who stay together make a conscious decision, based upon their marriage commitment, to plow through their problems together. Regardless of frustrations, disagreements, or personal foibles, they are determined to work things out—together. Problems are a part of life. Perhaps one of your life's greatest decisions will be, "Which set of problems do I want to live with?"

Second, couples who remain married must realize sooner or later (and the sooner the better) that many of their premarital impressions of marriage were little more than marital mush, the stuff of which myths and fairy tales are made. Some of these myths are handed down from our parents. We pick up others from friends, relatives, books, magazines, or movies. Regardless of their source, the sooner you dispel marital myths, the better chance you have for marital bliss!

In his book *Strike the Original Match* (Multnomah, 1980), expert preacher and respected author Charles R. Swindoll puts it this way:

> A harmonious marriage requires the continual destruction of myths. As fast as Hollywood can crank 'em out, married couples need to be able to assault and destroy those fantasies! A major myth of marriage is that it is a blissful, easygoing, relaxing cloud that floats from one restful day to the next. The guy who dreamed that one up should be *"shot at dawn."*

Many other myths surround the hazy, curious relationship known as marriage. Most of these myths are merely inconvenient nuisances on the road to marital intimacy. Many modern marriage myths are frivolous and foolish; some are harmless, humorous, or downright hilarious. But others are dangerous and destructive. They can drive a couple down from the mountaintop of newlywed delight to the valleys of disappointment, delusion, and despair and, if allowed to proceed unchecked, can plunge even the best relationship into the pit of divorce.

Many couples get into trouble early in their marriages because they regard their relationship as a treasure chest from which they can pluck rare gems at will. Actually, marriage is an empty box that must be continuously refilled.

J. Allan Petersen is a noted author and director of Family Concern, a ministry designed to bolster crumbling marriages and to help good marriages get better. Petersen says in an article in *Marriage Partnership* magazine (Spring 1989):

> Most people get married believing a myth—that marriage is a beautiful box full of all the things they have longed for: companionship, sexual fulfillment, intimacy, friendship. And that somehow the box mysteriously remains full of those goodies.
>
> After marriage, they start to empty the box, believing their spouse will fill it again. But it won't happen, at least not for long. The box gets empty, disappointment sets in, and the relationship takes a nosedive.

Can this process be avoided? Sure, but both of you have to put something *into* the box before you can get anything out of it. You need to sow love if you hope to reap a harvest of love. You can keep the box filled only by contributing large portions of loving, giving, forgiving, and serving each other. If you or your mate take more out than you put in, the box will soon be empty again.

How to Make Sure Your First Marriage Is Your Last

In this book, we want to explode some of the myths about marriage. We want to stick some pins in those hot-air balloons that have been bobbing along blissfully for years. Some of the "pops" and "bangs" you experience as you read may jolt you a bit, but keep in mind, couples who make their first marriage their last are those who deal with reality rather than those who float along in a world of illusion.

One of the best-kept lies of marriage must be this: "They got married and lived happily ever after." Does anybody really believe that? Even the most naive married person you can think of (and hopefully, it isn't you) knows in his or her heart that good marriages don't just happen. A good marriage takes work—lots of work!

Work? Yes, remember that worst of all the four-letter words? *W-O-R-K?* If you want a good marriage, it's going to take more than love. Whether you want to rekindle romance, build a loving relationship that lasts a lifetime, conquer incompatibility, overcome infidelity and keep your family from falling apart, or any combination of the above, it's going to take work. You either can work at it or watch your relationship wilt right before your eyes.

Some couples naively believe that if they have to work at their marriage, something must be wrong. Actually, the opposite is true. No matter how much you love each other, a good marriage will require incredible amounts of time, energy, and effort to be expended by both partners. But would you want it any other way? After all, a relationship that requires nothing is worth nothing.

Wonderful marriages don't simply blossom and bloom. They reek of "get down and dirty" work.

But what kind of work? What does it mean to *work* at a relationship? I hear you saying, "I know how to work at my job. I know how to work at cutting the grass, doing the laundry, or washing the car. But work at a relationship?" All through this book, I am going to give you practical suggestions that will help you work at your marriage and help your marriage work for you.

Come on along. Let's burst some balloons.

2
Turn On the Lights— the Party's Over!

Marriage Myth Number One:
The best surprise is no surprise. Or, "We won't have to adjust. We really *know* one another rather well . . . don't we?"

"The honeymoon is over when he phones to say he'll be late for supper and she's already left a note that it's in the refrigerator."

Bill Lawrence

● ● ● ● ● ● ● ● ● ● ● ● ● ●

Think back to your wedding day. Remember the excitement? The nervousness? The ceremony? The receiving line? The hugging, kissing, and crying? People were telling you how happy they were for you, and many of them honestly meant it! Most of your friends and relatives were thrilled that you were getting married. But over in the corner, not really entering into the festivities, stood a group who obviously did not belong at your wedding.

They were the philosophers. The skeptics.

As they approached you with clammy hands extended and pained looks on their faces, they offered feigned congratulations and advice.

"The first year is the hardest," said one.

"Marriage takes work," pontificated another.

"Keep her barefoot and pregnant and you'll be all right."

"It's all what you make of it," whispered Plato's long-lost progeny.

"If you can make it through all the wedding details, you can take almost anything life dishes out to you."

Yeah, sure. Believe that stuff and I've got some prize real estate for you down in you-know-where.

Regardless of how well prepared you were prior to saying "I do," just the fact that you are living with someone in such an intimate relationship as marriage creates previously unencountered problems and opportunities. No matter how well you knew your partner before your wedding, marriage, for most people, is a real shock to the system.

Latent in all of us are wonderful, weird, wacky qualities that mysteriously surface only within the relationship of marriage. Consequently, whatever your age and your reasons for marrying, your cultural and family backgrounds, or emotional makeup, there are issues that every married couple must face eventually: practical everyday questions about how you will spend your time, how you will handle money, the division of nitty-gritty household chores, as well as the weightier, more complex matters of physical, spiritual, and intellectual habits and growth. Often, such nitty-gritty concerns take newlyweds by surprise. A couple thinks, *Hey! We really do know each other. Right?* Wrong. Many new challenges and adjustments rear their heads right from the start, during the honeymoon. Some of those early adjustments hit you like a 250-pound chiropractor.

21

The Honeymooners

Ah, yes; the honeymoon. What a nice name for an experience that often resembles a grade C movie, *Tourists From Hell*. Think about it . . . *honeymoon*. The term usually conjures up images of a new husband and wife spending a relaxing vacation in some idyllic location, where they can enjoy their love unabashedly and enjoy an uninterrupted period of near-perfect, harmonious, pleasurable time together. Balmy days and intimate evenings are what the honeymoon is meant to be.

For some couples, though, the picture on the honeymoon hotel brochures and the pictures indelibly impressed upon their memories are radically different. Jeff and Suzanne had the first major fight of their marriage in a heart-shaped bathtub at a honeymoon resort in the Poconos. Suzanne wanted the water hotter; Jeff wanted it cooler. To cool him off, Suzanne dumped her ice-cold drink over Jeff's head. The bathtub water was not the only place where steam was rising that night.

Sometimes the best-laid honeymoon plans go awry due to unexpected developments, creating circumstances that force couples to take a crash course in "Marital Stress Management."

Mark and Diane had dreamed about every detail of their winter wedding in New York and their subsequent honeymoon in sunny Jamaica. When they arrived at the hotel just outside Montego Bay, they were disappointed to discover that their room had narrow single beds. Mark dutifully descended the eight stories to the lobby (the elevator was broken so he had to take the stairs). Once he was able to get the attention of the hotel manager, he lodged his complaint.

"We ordered a room with a double, full-size bed," he explained, "but the room you gave us has two single beds in it."

"Heh, heh. No problem," the Jamaican behind the counter responded. "Nice view, eh?"

"Well, yeah; sure. It's a beautiful view of the ocean, but my wife and I are on our honeymoon and we really would prefer a full-size bed."

"No problem," the manager repeated. "I take care of you. Go out, get some sun. When you come back from the beach, hah! You have double bed."

"Well, okay," Mark answered suspiciously, wondering why the manager didn't simply give them a different room. He trudged back up the eight flights of stairs and explained the situation to Diane. They changed into their bathing suits and headed for the beach.

The couple spent the entire afternoon frolicking in the warm, turquoise, Caribbean waters, while they waited for their room to be ready. At half-past four, the hotel manager finally reported to them that they now had a double bed in their room. But it was too late. The hot, tropical sun had already taken its toll on the lovebirds. They were burned to a scarlet-purple crisp.

That night, Mark and Diane could barely lie down on their double bed. Their bodies quaked with sunburn, sweating profusely one moment, shivering with cold the next. Anytime either of them touched the other, it sent searing, sizzling pain screaming across their skin. They attempted to sleep as far apart from each other as possible.

Throughout the night, they took turns emptying their stomachs into the commode.

The next day was worse. Huge welts appeared on their bodies from the blistering sunburn. Mark and Diane tried to eat, but they couldn't keep anything down.

The third day dawned and they were still sick.

The fourth day, they asked the hotel manager if he could return the single beds to their room.

Mark and Diane spent the rest of the week hurling accusations at each other.

"You should have double-checked the reservations," Diane blamed Mark.

"Yeah? Well, whose idea was it to spend all day in the sun?" Mark retorted.

"Oh! Pardon me. Who wanted to go to Jamaica anyhow? Not me! I wanted to go to a resort in the mountains, remember?"

Whew! What an awful way to start a marriage!

Obviously, it is impossible to prepare for such calamities. Nevertheless, couples are usually shocked to discover what a radical difference marriage makes in the way they relate to each other. According to Miriam Arond and Samuel L. Parker, authors of *The First Year of Marriage* (Warner, 1987), even partners who have lived together prior to being married are surprised to find that familiarity before marriage seems to have little to do with how easily a couple adapts within marriage.

Television doesn't help. Nowadays we are inundated with quick-fix solutions to even monumental problems. Nearly anything can be adjusted or remedied within a thirty-minute sitcom or a ninety-minute installment of a "minimisery series." If a couple is foolish enough to fall for such froth, they may quickly go from "The Dating Game" to "The Honeymooners" to "The Newlywed Game" to "Wheel of Fortune" to "Divorce Court"!

Marital happiness is not automatic, even when both partners love the Lord. It takes time to adjust to each other, to get used to doing things in new ways, to adapt, and to establish some sensible and satisfactory systems for living together as husband and wife. Maybe that's why, in biblical times, the honeymoon lasted at least one full year! Deuteronomy 24:5 declares, "When a man takes a new wife, he shall not go out with the army, nor be charged with any duty; he shall be free at home one year and shall give happiness to his wife whom he has taken."

Notice that the new husband received a military deferment and a break from business duties in order to spend quality time getting to know his bride. To make this possible, friends and family showered the newlyweds with enough money and presents that the husband didn't have to go to work! For one year, his top priority was getting to know and giving pleasure to his wife. Talk about a honeymoon!

Apparently, God intended that a couple's first year of marriage be set apart as a time for learning about, sharing with, and adapting to each other. In *The First Years of Forever* (Zondervan, 1988), noted physician and author Ed Wheat points out that the Hebrew word used in Deuteronomy 24:5 and rendered "to cheer up" or to "give happiness" means that the husband is "to delight his wife and to understand what is exquisitely pleasing to her in the sexual relationship." When God says He wants a married couple to get to know each other, He means *know* in the truest biblical sense!

Great Expectations

Getting married often changes what you expect from your mate and from yourself. Couples don't always verbalize such expectations, but consciously or unconsciously, they are there and adjustments are required. The experience of Jim and Marcy Garfield, a couple in their early thirties and married six years, exemplifies this curious phenomenon. Marcy complained:

> Before we got married, I never minded that Jim spent so much time with his friends, not doing anything constructive, just goofing off. After we were married awhile, I began to resent it. His job paid poorly and we were constantly scraping to make ends meet. I felt that if Jim would spend that time more wisely, he could go back to school and make something of himself. The odd thing to me is that I never was bothered by his laziness before we were married. But now, as his wife, I feel I'm entitled to expect better from Jim.

Fortunately for them, Jim realized that marriage required him to let go of his childish habits and take seriously his responsibilities as a husband. Thanks to Marcy's encouragement, he is now in his third year of dental school.

What are some of the more common unconscious expectations couples have of each other? Dr. Harvey L. Ruben, popular "Talknet" radio host, categorizes them under six groupings in *Supermarriage* (Bantam, 1986):

1. *Physical and emotional energy levels.* Many marriage partners simply march to a different drummer. Their metabolisms are different, their biological and psychological

rhythms are different; consequently, their energy levels are different. One may be winding down at 10:00 P.M. and the other has just gotten his or her second wind. If you and your spouse operate "out of sync," you might easily fail to meet each other's needs, simply because you lack the energy necessary to be there when your partner needs you.

2. *Sexual energy.* Every individual is unique in his or her sexual desire and need. But when one person has a high level of sexual energy and his or her partner has a low desire, great expectations can become a source of disillusionment and disappointment.

3. *Role playing.* By this, Dr. Ruben means the roles you watched your parents play as you were growing up. Their examples will determine, to a large degree, your expectations regarding your own marital roles.

4. *Intensity of interaction.* Again, much of this comes from the way you saw Mom and Dad interacting. Did your parents quietly discuss matters when a problem came up, or did they yell and scream, with one or both slamming the door and walking out? Did your folks spend their leisure time together or apart? Did they share responsibility for household chores?

However your mom and dad handled these areas has sifted down into your own unconscious expectations of your spouse. Certainly, you can choose to do things differently, but you at least need to be aware of the patterns that have preceded you.

5. *Emotional needs.* Everybody brings a certain amount of "emotional baggage" into the marriage relationship. Past hurts, hostilities, aggressive or passive behavior patterns all come with the person to whom you have com-

mitted yourself. If you are hoping that you or your spouse can heal these wounds without outside help, you may be expecting too much.

6. *Low self-esteem*. This may have worked against you in two possible ways: You may have been attracted to a person with high self-esteem in the hopes that your partner would buoy you up, or perhaps you were attracted to someone with a poor self-image in hopes that the two of you would understand each other's needs. When expectations are not met, you can become extremely discouraged if adjustments are not made in your marriage.

Understand, great expectations are not wrong; they are merely misguided. Each of us enters into marriage dreaming that the love and devotion of a good mate will satisfy all our needs. Of course, we don't say that aloud. People would laugh at us—especially people who have been married for a few years. Still, the expectations are there, and they can be harmful. But when you realize that your partner is only human, that he or she has shortcomings just as anybody else does, you can commit yourself to the delightful chore of establishing realistic expectations and adjusting to each other's real needs and desires.

Comedienne Sylvia Harney advises couples to take their marriage adjustments seriously but to laugh every chance they get. In discussing her own marital adjustments and expectations, she quipped, "After you marry you have to invent good reasons for things you never gave a second thought about before marriage. This man I married came out of the bathroom one evening and said, 'Is your bra on the towel rack for a reason?' I was prepared. 'Yes, it fits the towel rack better than it does me!' "

Sylvia observes in her book *Married Beyond Recognition* (Wolgemuth & Hyatt, 1988):

> We don't think about where we put our clothes be-
> fore marriage, but it can become the subject of a mas-
> ters thesis afterwards! Even if you have a good reason
> for hanging your bra on the towel rack, men don't
> understand. He never hangs *his* clothes on the towel
> rack. His never get that far off the floor! Most men
> don't even take the time to throw their clothes on the
> floor—they just let go and the force of gravity pulls
> them there.

Your attitude toward the adjustments you experience in your marriage will have a lot to do with how successful you are in adapting. By choosing to adjust rather than to adjourn, you are acknowledging that although you know each other extremely well, you and your partner still have a lot of room to grow.

When you discover that your expectations were based upon a myth or misinformation, it helps to keep your sense of humor. Roger and Nadine Johnson found this to be important.

One of the attributes that initially attracted Roger to his wife, Nadine, was her exquisite taste in clothing. All through their courtship, Nadine dressed as though she were a fashion model. Her apparel was always appropri-ate for the occasion; her hair stylishly set; makeup metic-ulously applied. Roger proudly walked arm-in-arm with his own personal fashion plate.

Then they got married. At home, on the first morning following the honeymoon, Nadine shuffled out of the bathroom dressed in an old, flannel robe and furry, fluffy slippers. She wore no makeup and her hair drooped and dangled down around her neck. Roger barely recognized his bride.

"Nadine!" he shouted. "What did you do to yourself?"

"What do you mean, Roger?"

"Why in the world are you dressed like that? Where are your good clothes, and why are you wearing those rags?"

"Well, I'm your wife now, Roger."

"So?"

"These are the kind of clothes my mom used to wear around the house," Nadine answered naively. "This is the way I always thought a good wife dressed."

"No, thanks, Nadine," Roger responded. "I want you to wear the same kind of clothes you wore before we got married." So much for family traditions.

Married life constituted quite an adjustment for my wife, Angela, and me. Prior to our meeting, we both had grown content with our singleness, adopting an attitude of "I think I will probably be single, but there is an outside chance that I may be married someday" rather than the more popular "I hope to get married, but there's a chance (God forbid!) that I may remain single." Because of our stubborn insistence upon singleness, it took God nearly three years to convince us we were ready for marriage!

We married on magnificent Mackinac Island in upper Michigan; honeymooned in heavenly Hawaii; then returned to coal-dust-ridden Clymer, Pennsylvania, to set up our tiny, three-room apartment, where we began "life in the real world."

Angela's Uncle Don had warned me about her cooking. A master of understatement, Don droned, "I don't want to say that Angela's cooking is bad, but last year, the flies took up a collection to get the hole in the screen door fixed!"

Inexperience notwithstanding (in other words, neither of us knew diddly about cooking), Angela and I were determined to establish our own traditions by basting and roasting our first Thanksgiving turkey in our brand-new, never-before-used oven.

We bought a beautiful bird. Big. Twenty pounds worth. Who cared that there were only two of us? Her folks or mine might drop in for leftovers.

Angela worked half the day on that turkey. She cleaned it, cut it, stuffed it and stuck it, painted it, and papered it. All the while, I stood by in adoring astonishment as my wife whittled, whacked, and walloped that bird. Finally, she squeezed "Big Bird" into a large baking pan and placed it in the oven. She set the timer and closed the oven door. The dastardly deed accomplished, it was time for bed.

> It was the night before Thanksgiving
> and all through the house,
> not a creature was stirring,
> not even a mouse. . . .

But around daybreak, a strange sound sporadically broke the silence.

"Psssst." It was coming from the oven.

"Pssssssssst." I heard it again.

"Psst; Angela," I said softly, as I shook her shoulder to gently wake her. "Did you hear that sound?"

"Huh? What sound?" she mumbled.

"Pssssssst," the turkey said again.

"There!" I shouted. "That sound! I think your turkey is boiling over." (Okay, okay. I told you I didn't know anything about cooking.)

"What?" Angela squealed, as she hopped out of bed and bolted out of the room. "Oh, no! Not my *turkey!*"

I quickly followed her into the kitchen, where smoke had already begun to billow out of the oven door. We whipped open the door, just in time to see the boiling hot grease bubbling over the rim of the roasting pan, splashing onto the hot oven floor, and igniting into blowtorch-type flames.

"My turkey!" Angela cried.

"Turkey, nothing," I shouted. "We're on fire!"

"No, no! I see what's wrong." Angela attempted to calm me. "The pan is too full. Let's lift it out and drain some of the grease off and it will be okay."

"Are you sure?"

"I think so."

"All right. Let's give it a try."

Unfortunately, in our haste to save the turkey, neither Angela nor I had taken note of the fact that we were both stark naked. The night before, we had delighted in celebrating our first Thanksgiving together in true newlywed fashion. Now, in the light of day, our nude bodies were no match for a boiling, fire-belching turkey.

As we carefully attempted to slide the turkey out of the oven without spilling the bubbling liquid, the boiling grease popped, splattering our naked bodies.

We tipped the pan.

Grease poured out of the baking pan, onto the oven floor, and erupted into flames. In a knee-jerk response, we yanked the turkey, pan and all, out of the oven and onto the floor. The fire followed the turkey.

Flames licked at our legs and smoke began to sting our eyes.

"Get the fire extinguisher!" Angela screamed.

Intuitively, I knew if we used the fire extinguisher, we could probably snuff out the flames, but we would also destroy our new stove, oven, and kitchen floor.

"No. Baking soda!" I answered.

"What?"

"There's baking soda in the refrigerator," I yelled to Angela as I attempted to keep the flames on the aluminum foil that had enfolded our turkey.

Angela ripped open the refrigerator door, found the baking soda, and in one motion, turned and sprayed the kitchen floor and the oven with the entire contents of the box.

The fire gasped for air, then disappeared.

Smoke, however, still filled our apartment and had begun to creep beneath our front door. My brother and his wife, who lived next door, noticed the smoke and began banging on the door. Angela and I quickly found our robes and unlocked the door.

"What's goin' on?" my brother asked calmly. "Is something on fire? Are you guys okay?"

"Yeah, we're all right," I replied, as I winced from the smoke in my eyes. "Happy Thanksgiving." I flipped a light switch to the "on" position. "Turn on the lights—the party's over!" The honeymoon was indeed over. This was "real life" now.

What makes adjusting to real life so difficult for many couples is their stubborn refusal to let go of the myth that

33

their marriage will be the world's first perfect union. Most people do not believe they *are* the perfect marriage partners. All but a few of us are too honest to be that arrogant. Nevertheless, many partners naively believe their union will bring together two imperfect creatures who will then *become* perfect through the marriage.

Such a dream! Unfortunately, some people marry a dream and wake up in a nightmare. Others simply refuse to wake up.

If you want to enjoy your marriage, a good place to begin is by accepting your partner "warts and all." You can accept and adjust to your partner without *condoning* everything he or she does, but you can also learn to accept and adjust without *condemning*.

Working at Adjustments

Contrary to the popular myth that purports, "If marriage partners truly know each other, their adjustments in marriage will be minor," every good marriage requires constant fine-tuning and adjustment. Here are some suggestions that will help with the process:

1. *Recognize that the spouse who now lives with you is the "real" person you married.* By now, most of the premarital facades have faded into oblivion. The person you dated and eventually married may have disappeared, as well. Okay, so you married a guy in a tux and you've been living with a dirty sweatshirt ever since. Maybe you didn't marry a beauty queen, a movie star, a famous musician, or a muscle-bound athlete—or maybe you did! Regardless, by now you have probably discovered that the celluloid image of perfection does not exist; you married your

spouse. Therefore, give up those myths and fantasies with which you entered into marriage; let go of the excess baggage that weighs you down. Accept your partner as he or she is, not how you anticipated he would be, and determine to make the most of your marriage. As the saying goes, "If God gives you lemons, make lemonade!"

2. *Realize that marriage does not magically solve all of life's problems.* In fact, it normally precipitates more problems, all of which require a measure of adjustment in order to solve. Still, it is possible to choose joy in the midst of adjustments.

3. *Strengthen your image as a couple.* The two of you have become one flesh, as the Bible says (Genesis 2:24). As such, it is important that you begin to perceive yourselves as one, not merely as two individuals who happen to be sharing the same bathroom facilities. Certainly, you are two distinct personalities, and marriage should not suppress or subjugate either you or your spouse. But you are also two who have willingly committed yourselves to being one: the Smiths, the Walkers, the Bakers. Think, see, and talk "couple talk" rather than "yours" and "mine," and never allow parents, children, or other people to pit you against each other.

4. *Establish positive patterns in your marriage.* When you married, you and your spouse started a new life together. You have the opportunity to cultivate new and different behavior patterns in this relationship; you need not duplicate the past. Your marriage partnership is one that has never previously existed. Therefore, you can establish your own priorities, celebrations, and traditions, even if it means burning the Thanksgiving Day turkey, as Angela

and I did. Incidentally, we have decided to eliminate that tradition from further celebrations.

5. *Don't try to change your partner by nagging, complaining, cajoling, or coercing.* I once overheard a dear woman expressing a prayer I knew God would not answer. She prayed, "You love my husband, Lord, and I'll change him!" She has the process precisely backwards. The Lord has commanded *us* to do the loving of our marriage partners, and *He* will do the changing. The Bible says it is the Holy Spirit's job to convict of sin, righteousness, and judgment (John 16:8). It is not your responsibility to change your mate. Don't attempt to be your partner's "personal Holy Spirit." He or she already has One.

Your responsibility is to take care of you, to keep your attitude positive and your actions biblical, allowing the Lord to make you an instrument through which His love may flow, thus becoming a catalyst for constructive change in your partner.

Psychologists Melvin Kinder and Connell Cowan state in their book *Husbands and Wives* (Potter, 1989), "Change in a marriage is possible, but it will never happen so long as you make it something your mate should be doing." Kinder and Cowan, authors of such bestselling books as *Smart Women/Foolish Choices* and *Women Men Love/Women Men Leave*, believe the only effective method of changing your marriage partner begins with you. The psychologists acknowledge that most people hate the thought of having to give up pushing their mates to change, even when they know such efforts have met with failure and more frustration. Nevertheless, it is only as we abandon useless attempts to change our mates and instead focus on our own attitudes and actions that positive changes begin to take place in our partners.

6. *Never assume anything!* Sure, you know each other extremely well. But in any relationship, it is always wise to clearly spell out your expectations. When your spouse disappoints you or you find that your expectations are not being met, search your memory bank, asking, "Did we agree to do things that way, or did I just assume that's the way it would be?" If you and your partner have agreed to a particular pattern, either tactfully confront your spouse and remind him or her of your agreement, or establish a new deal.

Before you pop your cork, though, consider this: Maybe you simply *assumed* that she wouldn't mind if you went bowling every Friday night, or that he would be delighted to go shopping every Saturday afternoon.

Speak up. As best you can, communicate what you are thinking and feeling on the inside. Remember, your marriage partner is not a mind reader.

7. *Don't be afraid or embarrassed to ask for help.* Because the need to adjust to each other is so real in even the best of relationships, it should not surprise us when problems arise in the early years of marriage. In addition, couples whose problems do not surface until much later in the relationship frequently can trace the source of their irritation back to the initial phases of their marriage. Unfortunately, an unwritten code often keeps couples from seeking help during those formative stages. Society implies that almost anybody with half a brain can make it through the blissful early years of marriage.

"Don't worry, be happy," society sings.

"Just let them alone and they will work it out," many

people comment about couples who are struggling with marital stress.

The message cuts through all the smiles, loudly and clearly communicating, "Don't call us, we'll call you. Don't sweat the small stuff. Whenever you have a *real* problem, after you've tried everything else, then it is appropriate to seek counsel." This misconception foisted upon couples is not only foolish and false, it is also unbiblical and counterproductive. The Bible repeatedly encourages us to seek wise counsel: "The way of a fool is right in his own eyes, But a wise man is he who listens to counsel" (Proverbs 12:15).

The writer of Proverbs also says, "Listen to counsel and accept discipline, That you may be wise the rest of your days. Many are the plans in a man's heart, But the counsel of the Lord, it will stand" (Proverbs 19:20, 21).

To ignore sources of wisdom and encouragement during the early days of your marriage is to flirt with divorce. Marcia Lasswell says in an article in *Medical Aspects of Human Sexuality* (February 1985), "Researchers report that nearly half of all serious marital problems develop in the first two years of marriage. Yet, on the average, couples who seek counseling for the first time have already been married seven years."

Did you catch the significance of that statement? Many couples continue to slide downhill in their relationships for *five years* or more before seeking help! Many of those who do seek help have ignored the warning signals for far too long. Often, it takes something drastic, such as a separation, a threat of divorce, or an extramarital affair to shock the couple into seeking advice.

Avoid this mess. At the first sign of serious trouble, seek

wise counsel from an objective, Bible-believing source you respect. Your pastor can help; sometimes a professional psychologist or marriage counselor may be necessary. Parents and friends who counsel you from a biblical basis can also be a great blessing, although it is only natural that they may be prejudiced in your behalf. Whatever you do, don't allow a downhill slide to continue in your marriage because you are afraid of what other people might think or say. Church gossips and backyard speculators can whisper about you all they want, but only you can take the positive action needed to revive your marriage.

8. *Adopt a Serenity Prayer attitude about your marriage.* The well-known prayer says, "God grant me the courage to change the things I can change, the serenity to accept those things I cannot change, and the wisdom to know the difference."

Speaking of differences . . . wow! Are there ever some mythological whoppers floating around in those clouds! Let's see if we can answer this age-old question: "Why are men so strange and women so weird?"

3
Toilets, Toothpaste, and Other Tidbits

Marriage Myth Number Two:
Two married people will be alike in their personal habits and tastes. Or, "Our differences don't matter that much, do they?"

"There are two times when a man doesn't understand a woman—before marriage and after marriage."

"Keep your eyes wide open before marriage, half shut afterwards."

Ben Franklin

● ● ● ● ● ● ● ● ● ● ● ● ●

Men and women are different. Oh? You noticed? No, no. I mean *really* different! At times, I question whether Angela and I are even of the same species. We're that different.

Obviously, males and females differ anatomically. Carol Ann Rinzler, quoted in *Marriage Partnership* magazine (Winter 1989), says a man's hands normally are larger than a woman's. So is his nose. Because of the male Y chromosome, a man's ears are hairier than those of a woman. And although you may not believe it, a woman's armpits are normally smellier than a man's, due to a fatty substance that is secreted from glands under her arms. These substances are digested by bacteria and their by-products create the foul aroma.

Women live longer than men, according to most statistics. A schoolteacher once asked her fourth-grade class to explain this phenomenon. After a few moments of stymied silence, a little boy in the back of the room began flailing his arms.

"I know! I know, teacher," he squealed, barely able to contain his enthusiasm.

"Okay. Tell us, Ricky. Why do women usually live longer than men?"

"Because they don't have wives!" the boy answered.

I know some married men who would concur with the kid.

Basically, the differences that exist between you and your spouse can be divided into two types: those that can be changed, and those that cannot be helped. The first type includes differences that are realistically resolvable. For example, you are a night owl who enjoys staying up to watch television and then sleeping late the following morning, but your mate is a morning person who wants to wake up at the first glimmer of dawn's early light. Not a simple problem, but it is not insurmountable, either. With a bit of compromise, the two of you can settle on some equitable solution.

The second sort of differences can't be solved so easily, and many cannot be changed at all. Contrasts attributable to your birth, family background, age, race, height, appearance, and other personal characteristics lend little opportunity for change. Certainly, some of these differences can be overlooked or overcome, but their influence and ramifications are bound to pop up in your marriage.

In fact, in almost every marriage, it's only a short period of time before one or both partners figure out, "One of us is really weird!"

Strange, isn't it? When you first met your mate, you felt blessed to have finally found someone who understood you, who shared your likes and dislikes, your values and goals, who was so downright compatible with you. Then, somewhere between saying "I do" and saying "You what?" those same qualities that initially attracted you to each other turned into annoyances that trigger attack missiles.

What complicates matters more is that people with opposite personality traits often find each other extremely attractive. Mark Twain observed that there are two kinds of people in this world: one who is always ten minutes early, and another who is always ten minutes late. Furthermore, Twain added sardonically, "They're always married to each other!"

Opposites do attract. They click as a couple because they complement each other. After a while, they say, "Hey, this is really working! Let's get married." The quiet, subdued, passive person then marries the loud, dynamic, controlling person; the spontaneous, irresponsible person marries a more stable and conservative type; the neatnik marries the slovenly. Then each person proceeds to pursue the prime purpose of marriage: attempting to change his or her partner into a reproduction of himself or herself!

Quirks That Drive Couples Crazy

Some differences between marriage partners are simply silly, insignificant idiosyncrasies, but others are quirks that can drive a couple crazy! Being aware of this, I decided it would be better for Angela and me to settle some serious matters right at the beginning of our marriage.

We had hardly gotten home from our honeymoon when I called Angela into the living room.

"Please sit down, Angela," I said in a somber tone of voice. "I want to set some things straight."

"What is it, Ken?" Angela answered demurely. She sat down and prepared for a serious discussion.

I took a deep breath before speaking, then boldly launched into my spiel: "Do you like the commode seat *up*, or do you prefer to keep the commode seat *down*?"

"Do I what?" Angela asked, as she convulsed in laughter.

"You heard me. Seat up or seat down?" I repeated with a straight face.

"Well, I, er, I don't know!" She sputtered through her laughter.

"Come on now; make up your mind," I pressured her.

"Down!" she decided quickly and then lost it again, as her laughing brought tears to her eyes.

"Okay. Next question. Do you like to squeeze the toothpaste from the top, or do you want to roll it up from the bottom?" I pressed.

"I like to squeeze it from the middle," Angela replied straightforwardly, wiping her eyes as she answered.

"Mmm." I hadn't considered that option, but I was a better man now that I knew.

What does such nonsense have to do with maintaining a happy marriage? Maybe not much . . . for some folks. But for others, those tiny, seemingly insignificant matters rapidly grow into annoyances that can knock them for a loop.

Rudy and Claudia, a couple who have been married for seventeen years, told me that one of the battles of their marriage has been whether the toilet paper should hang *over* the rest of the roll or *under* the roll. It may not matter to you, but every time one of them replaces the tissue incorrectly, the roll is nearly called "up yonder."

Lisa and Kurt get all heated up over how many blankets to keep on their bed at night. Lisa complains, "I'm real cold-blooded. I feel as if I'm freezing all the time, especially my feet! Kurt could go out hunting in just a flannel shirt and be quite cozy. When we go to bed, I like at least three heavy blankets on us; sometimes more in the winter. Kurt wants to sleep with only a sheet covering us. A couple of times, I've gotten so angry over this, I've told him to go ahead and sleep with his sheet—on the couch!"

Can We Ever Get to Church on Time?

I am a schedule maniac. Most of my life has been governed by a clock, an appointment book, or a calendar. To me, it is not cleanliness but punctuality that is next to godliness. I'd rather be thirty minutes early than two minutes late.

I'm not certain Angela owned a watch before she met me. To her, time is an inconvenient human limitation infringing upon the vastness of eternity. Her attitude is, "Hey, we're going to live forever! What's a few minutes here or there?" It's tough to argue with that kind of logic.

Although I have never seen a survey to substantiate this statement, I believe Sunday morning is the worst part of the week for many Christian couples—especially those with young children. In the early years of Angela's and my marriage, every Sunday morning started much the same way. I'd wake up and start whining about going to church.

"I'm not going to church today," I'd say, putting the pillow over my head.

"Come on, Ken; you have to go," Angela would gently chide.

"No, I don't want to go. The people at that church don't like me. Nobody listens to me when I talk, and I feel certain they go out and say horrible things about me behind my back. I don't need that. I'm gonna stay right here in 'Bedside Baptist.' "

"Ken, you have to go. You're the *pastor!*"

So we'd get up and get ready to go to church, which, as every married person knows, sounds a lot easier than it really is! Especially for us. Our church was over an hour's drive from home. That meant we had to get up in the middle of Saturday night in order to get cleaned up, have breakfast, and outsmart the state police on the way to worship service. Have you ever been on "Mr. Toad's Wild Ride" at Disney World or Disneyland? Sundays at our place felt similar to that.

We tried various methods of time management. We shuffled the shower schedule: Angela showered while I shaved; she showered before me; I'd shower before her; we'd shower together. (We almost missed the entire service that time!) Nothing helped.

We'd lay our clothes out on Saturday night, only to decide to wear something else on Sunday morning. We even attempted to overcome the Sunday-morning madness by staying overnight at a motel near the church! More mayhem.

During the early years of our marriage, we did okay. We never missed a Sunday-morning service. I do recall, however, several Sundays when our Chrysler New Yorker miraculously seemed to sprout wings and turn into a stealth bomber, zooming past police radar undetected. I reasoned it was all right to break the speed laws. After all, it was for the ministry (I later repented).

Angela and I had just about established a workable Sunday-morning routine, getting out of bed at 5:30 A.M. in order to arrive in time for our church's 10:30 A.M. service. Then Ashleigh was born.

Prior to the birth of our daughter, Angela and I loved to travel together. On a whim, we'd pack up and take off on some new adventure. After Ashleigh, it took a major effort merely to make it to church! Before Ashleigh, I had grown accustomed to grabbing my suit coat in one hand, my Bible and sermon in the other, and kicking the door shut as Angela and I exited our apartment.

With the advent of Ashleigh, I now had fourteen trips to make to the car before departure time. We had to have the diaper bag. Had to have a car seat. We couldn't possibly leave without an extra blanket. How about the stroller? Ashleigh's toys? Whew! I was tired before we ever got to church. I almost fell asleep during my own sermon!

Meanwhile, as I trekked back and forth to the car, Angela was feverishly attempting to get Ashleigh ready for church. (Why is it that babies always become cantankerous when you are trying to hurry?) I did my best to help by getting into the car, setting the heat or air-conditioning levels, turning on the radio, and then honking the horn.

Nowadays, we do get to church on time, but I must admit I have a much deeper empathy for those members of the congregation who pull into the church parking lot with their windows all steamed up. When I see them, I know a mysterious metamorphosis has already begun to take place.

In a matter of minutes, they have gone from, "Eat your cereal, you ungrateful little squirt" to "Get in the car, right now!" to "If you touch that window one more time, I'm gonna break your fingers!" to "Good morning, pastor! God bless you!" Who says the age of miracles is past?

But We Knew Each Other Before We Were Married

In counseling sessions, I often hear couples say, "We were so much alike before we got married. What happened?" Part of the answer is that love is blind but marriage is not. Occasionally, couples get married without being aware of their differences in religion, politics, communication skills, values, goals, or ideas about fun and family. More often, it is not that you didn't see those quirky qualities in your spouse before you got married; you did not *want* to see those kinks, cracks, or idiosyncrasies. That's why premarital counseling is often ineffective.

Please don't misunderstand. I am a strong advocate of premarital counseling, but usually it's like trying to put a "caution" sign up in the middle of Niagara Falls. Once a couple becomes engaged, they tend to be swept along toward taking the plunge. Everything centers on the wedding arrangements and there is little evaluation of the relationship.

It's tough to tell an engaged couple about toilet seats, toothpaste, and other tidbits. In the first place, they are only semiconscious when they come in for premarital counseling. They are so much in love. When I begin to talk about their different attitudes or past practices involving family, money, communication, or sex, most lovers stare at me with that glazed look in their eyes, as though they had just seen Grizzly Adams eaten alive by Teddy Ruxpin.

They do listen with interest when I talk to them about sex. Unfortunately, they are so swept up in their passion, they refuse to focus on anything other than the positive traits they see in each other.

While I appreciate their positive attitudes, a strong dose of reality could save them a lot of hassles later on in marriage. The truth is that men and women are attracted by their opposite characteristics, but normally they marry because of what they have in common. This practice prompted popular speaker and author Florence Littauer to quip at a seminar, "We marry a person for their assets and end up living with their deficits."

The Person I'm Married to Isn't the Person I Married!

Before you were married, when you and your spouse were "courting" each other, it seemed foolish to focus upon foibles. After all, why concentrate on the negatives? But once you were "hitched" and the rose-colored glasses came off, those quirky habits began to haunt you. It was relatively easy to tolerate your loved one's weird ways while you were dating, but when you began to realize you had committed yourself to living with those eccentricities for the rest of your life, you were spooked!

Why is this? Why do people change so much after they are married? Certainly, part of the answer lies with our naivete. But beyond that, two other possibilities exist: One, most couples tend to "let down their hair" a little after they are legally married. This can be good or bad. Some couples feel more comfortable with each other; others get lazy. After marriage, they may not feel they need to be so polite to each other, or they may become lax in personal discipline.

For example, why do many men and women put on weight after they get married? My brother told me it was "contentment fat."

"You wait," he said, "you'll see. After you get married, you'll put on ten to fifteen pounds. It's from being content."

"But I *am* content already," I protested.

"You'll see."

I got married and immediately put on ten pounds. Maybe it was contentment; maybe it was because I indulged in a bowl of ice cream every night before bed. Regardless, I knew I was in trouble when our small-town cop accused Angela of being a polygamist. He said, "Lady, you married one guy, but you're living with another!"

My insurance man added insult to injury. He said, "Ken, if you're going to keep eating like that, we'll have to get you a *group* life insurance policy!"

I substituted popcorn for ice cream and dropped the ten pounds.

Many couples feel less compelled to impress each other once they are married. They are often more secure and therefore more relaxed. This can develop a delightful "naturalness" between you, but beware of sloppiness, complacency, lack of discipline, or other childish habits. Determine to give your mate your best.

The second reason people often change radically after marriage is the result of realizing what really matters. Marriage does strange things to people. Often, it forces them to reevaluate their values and beliefs. This frequently shows up in the spiritual areas of life. Take the case of Michelle and Rob. He told me:

> Michelle never mentioned going to church *before* we were married. But a few months after our wedding, she started to get real religious. She didn't want to party anymore. She quit drinking alcoholic beverages and became insistent that I do the same. I said, "Hey, babe, if you don't want to drink, that's up to you. But don't push your religion onto me."
>
> When we started having kids, she really flipped out. Suddenly, it was important to take the kids to church all the time. This religion thing has really divided us. I feel as if I'm being left out of my own family.

Maybe Michelle did not realize spiritual matters would become so important to her, but she, like many others, quickly discovered that marriage, family, and spiritual life belong together. Marriage has the potential to bring the best out of people, causing them to change for the better. In Michelle's life, that is what happened. Unfortunately, Rob didn't see it that way.

Why Is My Mate So Weird?

My personal philosophy is this: "Everybody's beautiful in their own way . . . and everybody's *weird* in their own way." Okay, so it's not all that profound, but it does provide a certain tolerance of other people's peccadilloes. This is an especially helpful premise when you are approaching marriage matters.

Many of the differences that cause trouble and resentment in marriage come right out of those mythological marital expectations. If you are like most people, you probably brought into your marriage some specific ideas about what you expect to get from your spouse and what you are willing to give. If you received wise counsel before you got married, somebody encouraged you to discuss those expectations honestly and frankly with each other. Most couples did not.

Consequently, when your spouse doesn't live up to your expectations, even if you've never communicated them, you feel as though you've been ripped off. As a result, bitterness breeds.

For example, you may find yourself frequently criticizing your mate for wasting money, while you are attempting to save frugally for your future together. Part of the reason you feel hurt, angry, or betrayed is that your expectations of your spouse were that he or she would be a reliable, considerate business partner with you. When those expectations are not met, resentment can creep into your relationship.

One of the most common reasons Christian couples become extremely disillusioned and discouraged with each other is that one partner fails to live up to the other's spiritual expectations. Natalie and Steve are a classic example.

Steve claimed to be a Christian when they married, but Natalie was never sure whether his commitment was to Christ or to her. Natalie had expected that she was marrying a man of God, a man upon whom she could lean for spiritual strength and a man whose spiritual leadership she could trust. Within weeks after the wedding, she realized she was wrong.

Although Steve was interested in the spiritual realm of their relationship, that was not his first priority. His job came first, then his golf game. Then his friends. While he constantly assured Natalie that she topped his priority list, she doubted his word. "How could I be that important to him, when the things I am most concerned about in life are hardly even significant to Steve?"

Steve was glad to go to church with Natalie on Sunday mornings—as long as he got to go golfing on Sunday afternoons. Natalie, however, found that offensive; her views of keeping the Sabbath did not include playing golf on Sunday. She wanted to go back to church on Sunday evening, but Steve rarely returned from the course in time. When he did arrive before service time, he was "too tired to go listen to the preacher." After a while, Natalie began going alone.

Something similar happened to their times of prayer and Bible reading. Steve never initiated such practices before they were married, though he always placated Natalie's notions about spiritual unity that she supposed resulted from their studying the Scripture and praying together. After they were married, Steve found even more excuses not to pick up a Bible or to pray with his wife.

Although their marriage has continued to exist, Natalie is frustrated and baffled. "I can't *make* him be spiritual," she lamented.

Natalie is right. She can't force Steve to function as the spiritual leader of their family. He has to want to do that himself. Natalie can only encourage Steve to seek the Lord first in his life.

Her expectations are not the problem. She has every right to keep her spiritual standards high and uncompromising. On the other hand, nagging and complaining will only drive a wedge between Steve and Natalie, while reducing his desire to be a godly man. Natalie must adjust her spiritual expectations to the reality of Steve's spiritual maturity. Certainly, she should also pray for Steve and, if possible, pray *with* him. When one partner is spiritually more mature than his or her mate, short, sentence-type prayers together are often more effective than long, awkward attempts at prayer. If nothing else, Natalie could ask Steve each day as he leaves for work, "What would you like for me to pray about for you today?" It is important to keep prayer as one of the foundation stones upon which the marriage is built.

Body Language

In their book *The Language of Love* (Focus, 1988), Gary Smalley and John Trent suggest that the differences between the male and female approaches to life are fundamentally physical in nature. Basing their conclusions upon Dr. Richard Restak's book *The Brain* and Robert Goy's work, *Sexual Differentiation of the Brain*, Smalley and Trent explain:

Medical studies have shown that between the eighteenth and twenty-sixth week of pregnancy, something happens that forever separates the sexes. Using heat-sensitive color monitors, researchers have actually observed a chemical bath of testosterone and other sex-related hormones wash over a baby boy's brain. This causes changes that never happen to the brain of a baby girl.

This, researchers believe, causes most (but not all) boys to be more left-brain oriented and most (but not all) girls to be apt to use both the right and left hemispheres of the brain. Because the left brain houses more of the logical, analytical, factual, and aggressive patterns of thought, Smalley and Trent conclude:

It enjoys conquering five hundred miles a day for family vacation trips; favors mathematical formulas over Harlequin romances; stores the dictionary definition of love; and generally favors clinical, black-and-white thinking. It's the side of a man's brain that can't wait to buy the latest copy of some how-to magazine for the latest fix-it technique; memorizes batting averages and box scores; and loves to sit for hours, watching back-to-back games and yelling at referees.

On the other hand, most women spend the majority of their days and nights camped out on the right side of the brain . . . the side that harbors the center for feelings, as well as the primary relational, language, and communication skills; enables them to do fine-detail work; sparks imagination; and makes an afternoon devoted to art and fine music actually enjoyable. It pulls over at rest stops and historical markers on purpose; doesn't vaguely care about football or hockey games unless they know the players or their wives; stores and expresses the feelings of love, not just the definition; and would rather read *People* than *Popular Mechanics*.

Obviously, these basic mental differences can wreak havoc when it comes to communication between the sexes. Smalley and Trent suggest that the best way to bridge the gap between the genders is by building "emotional word pictures" comprised of descriptive or illustrative material that taps into the other person's emotions, experience, or understanding.

Personality Plus . . . or Minus?

Some differences couples encounter are due to personality types. It would do every married couple good to sit down with a competent counselor and take some basic personality tests such as the "Taylor-Johnson Temperate Analysis," the "Myers-Briggs Type Indicator" test, or the "Personal Profiles System" test. Don't let the big names scare you. Although a qualified person must administer these exams and explain the results, the tests are simple, fun, enlightening, and best of all, there are no right or wrong answers—only answers that are true for *you*. A biblical version of "Personal Profiles" can even help you discover the Bible characters and their personality traits to whom you are most similar!

Of course, testing instruments are only tools a counselor can use to help you better understand yourself or your mate. Still, a closer look at your personality traits may reveal volumes about your approach to life, which may or may not be similar to that of your spouse.

My good friend and co-worker Dr. David Chilcote admitted that these tests helped save his marriage to his wife, Marlene. For nearly thirty years, they lived together in silent frustration about their differences, each not able to understand why the other acted so strangely. Often, in the middle of a conversation, David would simply stand up, excuse himself, and walk away. He would go upstairs, read a book, or just spend some time alone. Several hours later, he would return, ready to talk again.

David's odd disappearances nearly drove Marlene nuts! Whenever her husband suddenly decided he was finished talking, she would sit aghast, wondering, *Well, what's wrong with me? Did I say or do something to offend David?* Since she was not the strong, silent type, Marlene frequently called after her husband in less-than-complimentary terms.

Then one day, just for the fun of it, Marlene and David took a "Myers-Briggs" personality test. The results shocked the couple. To their amazement, they discovered that David is an introvert and Marlene is an extrovert. While Marlene loves to be around other people for hours on end, David can interact only for small segments of time before he needs a break to be by himself. Otherwise, he feels cooped up, trapped, and irritable.

Suddenly, after thirty years of marriage, David and Marlene began to understand each other in a new way; they each began to accept why the other partner behaves as he or she does. Now, rather than reacting negatively to David's need for solitude, Marlene encourages him to "go take a walk." On the other hand, David recognizes Marlene's need for conversation and interaction with other people and encourages her participation in community and church activities. A simple analysis and acceptance of their basic personality differences has worked wonders in their marriage.

How to Quit Quibbling Over Quirks

I promised to provide you with practical pointers to help you understand how you can work at your marriage. Here are five simple suggestions that can help you adjust to some of the differences between you and your mate.

1. *Try to understand where your spouse is coming from.* The technical word for this is *empathy*. Empathy is more than sympathy. It is putting yourself in the other person's place, trying to feel what he or she feels, walking a mile in your mate's shoes.

Once when I suggested this principle to a wife who was estranged from her husband, the woman snapped back, "I've smelled his shoes and I wouldn't step within a mile of them, let alone walk a mile in them!" You win some; you lose some.

2. *Concentrate on your similarities rather than your differences.* Obviously, you had some things in common before you got married. What were they? Music? Movies? Golf? Old houses? Renew your acquaintance with some of those shared interests.

3. *Learn to appreciate your partner's differences, and don't be bashful about expressing that appreciation.* I am an analytical, conservative person by nature, but I am married to a woman who is more spontaneous and expressive. From time to time, I remind Angela that I appreciate her pulling me away from my desk, getting me out of the office and off

on an unplanned excursion. She in turn lets me know she appreciates my stability and thoughtful decisions. We complement each other. Keep in mind, too, that quirks and creativity often coexist. Henry Ford, the auto king, was both a creative tinkerer who loved to stick his head under the hood of an old tractor and an eccentric who had more than thirty birdbaths installed around his Michigan mansion. All of the birdbaths were heated. Quirky? You bet. But what a creative genius Ford was, as well!

4. *Agree to disagree.* Sometimes when differences create tension, you can compromise. At other times, you can't. When compromise seems impossible, rather than argue, blame, or criticize, it is often best to simply disagree in love. By an act of your will, acknowledge your love, acceptance, and respect for your spouse despite your differences. After all, those differences were probably part of what attracted you to each other in the first place!

5. *Explore your family tree.* You may be surprised to learn what runs in your family or in your spouse's family. Some of your differences are hereditary; some were adopted from other family members. Regardless, you didn't marry only a person; you married an entire family. Which brings us to another interesting myth about marriage. . . .

4
Mother-in-Law Mayhem

Marriage Myth Number Three:
Good Christians never have in-law problems.
Or, "Hey! I married *you*, not your whole family!"

"When it comes to broken marriages, most husbands will split the blame—half his wife's fault, and half her mother's."

"Do not insult the mother alligator until after you have crossed the river."

Haitian Proverb

"Happiness is having a large, loving, caring, close-knit family in another city."

George Burns

● ● ● ● ● ● ● ● ● ● ● ● ● ●

Perhaps no other area of a couple's relationship can create such emotional trauma as stress between or about each other's families. Like it or not, your family has been and will continue to be important to you—and your spouse probably feels the same way about his or her family. All well and good, until relatives—regardless of their intentions—try to intervene in your marriage. That's when in-laws can become outlaws.

The problem often intensifies because what seems like normal, loving concern to you may smack of intrusiveness to your mate (or vice versa). Denny and Laura found this out the hard way.

Since the first Sunday after they returned from their honeymoon nineteen years ago, Denny has insisted that he and Laura eat Sunday dinner with his parents. Actually, Denny's parents made it plain that they *expected* the newlyweds to participate in this family tradition they had inherited from *their* parents. Consequently, every week, immediately following church services, which they attend with Denny's parents, Denny and Laura dutifully collect their children and head to Grandma and Grandpa's house for dinner.

Denny's mom always cooks a delicious meal, but the whole ordeal chafes Laura so badly she can barely eat a bite.

"I appreciate their kindness," Laura lamented, "and it does make things a lot easier on me. I work all week, and not having to prepare Sunday dinner is a luxury in a way. But it's the fact that we feel *obligated* to go that gets me.

"Denny's parents just don't understand—or won't understand—that their son has other obligations now. Their demands that we attend Sunday dinner are like refusing to recognize their son is married and has a family of his own. They just won't let go!

"Every week Denny and I pledge to each other that we won't go this time; I have even cooked meals ahead of time and had our dinner ready at home. But then after church his parents say, 'See you out at the house,' and we follow their car like children following the Pied Piper. I get angry with Denny for not standing up to his parents. He defends them, and we end up fighting like cats and dogs almost every Sunday night."

To Denny, his parents are being kind, helpful, and considerate. To Laura, they are intruding and driving a wedge between Denny and her.

Torn Between Two Loves

Why is such uneasiness concerning in-laws so common and so disconcerting? Let's face it: your attachment to your parents and siblings may appear to be much stronger than the ties to your marriage partner. After all, if you grew up in your parents' home, you spent some of the most important years of your life under their watchful eyes. In most cases, you still want to please them. Even though you are married, you want to maintain family loyalties. That's why there is so much truth to the old saying, "In every marriage, there are at least six people—the wife, the husband, and the two parents of each."

When anything threatens your relationship with your family, you automatically recoil. If your partner says anything critical of your relatives, you are personally offended. At the same time, you may purposely avoid becoming close with your spouse's family for fear that your getting along too well with your in-laws may be perceived as disloyalty by your own relatives. It's a catch-22; either way you go, you lose. But it doesn't have to be that way.

From your parents' and your in-laws' perspective, your marriage presents a different set of problems. You often hear the phrase, "I didn't lose a daughter; I gained a son" (or vice versa). In many cases, parents and in-laws are quick to spout this obligatory platitude but mighty slow to believe it. You will always be your parents' little boy or girl. Similarly, to some extent, your spouse will always be an outsider to your parents, as you will be to your partner's parents.

It is understandable that your parents will probably be supersensitive about and overcritical of your partner. It may take them some time to appreciate the qualities in your mate that appear quite obvious to you. Likewise, as the son-in-law or daughter-in-law, you will initially pose a sort of threat to your spouse's family. You are the one who has "stolen" their child away from them.

In-law problems can be met and conquered if the six people involved in your marriage will realize that with a few puffs of air on your wedding day, when you and your partner said, "I do," immediately your prime allegiances transferred from your parents to each other. You made a commitment to each other which supersedes your loyalties to your parents. You decided to establish your own family; as such, you should never feel disloyal or ungrateful about shifting your allegiance to your spouse.

Practically, this means you will spend less time with your parents and siblings and more time with your partner. It means you must make it clear to any and all intruders that you and your mate desire time alone. It may also mean giving up some family traditions you and your spouse have enjoyed for years in order to establish your own traditions. Certainly love, respect, honor, and devotion can still be expressed to each of your families, but never in ways that are destructive to your marriage relationship.

Dealing With a Meddlesome Mother-in-Law

"I just can't take it anymore!" Paula shouted as she stormed into my office, literally pulling at her hair.

"Whoa! Whoa! Take it easy. What's going on?" I asked as I ushered her to a chair. "What's the matter?"

"That woman! She makes me want to scream!"

"What woman?" I asked, still confused. "Who are you talking about?"

"Scott's mother." Paula pronounced the words as if she were trying to expel a mouthful of Listerine. "She's always butting in, trying to tell me the *right* way to do things, trying to show me how *she* always took care of dear, little Scotty. Well, I've had it with her! Do you know what she's doing right now?"

"Ah . . . no, I haven't the foggiest idea," I answered, smiling in an attempt to disarm the distraught woman.

"She's doing my washing," Paula replied.

"See there; she's not such a bad woman."

"Oh, no? I already *did* the washing." Paula's words spun out of her mouth. "But the sheets weren't white enough, so Wonder Woman decided to do them again. In *my* house. She's doing *my* laundry over again, in *my* washer! Who does she think she is, anyhow?"

"Wonder Woman?" I repeated.

"She lives across town, and she stops by every time she 'happens' to be in the neighborhood—which is almost every afternoon around four o'clock. Scott gets home about six, but by the time he arrives, I'm snorting steam out my nose, because of his mom. For two solid hours, she picks, picks, picks. 'There's dust on the television, Paula,' she says; then she gets a rag and wipes it off. 'Oh, my! Are your dishes still in the sink?' She washes them. The other day, she cleaned out our underwear drawers!

"When Scott comes home, she turns into the perfect mother-in-law, helpful yet not pushy. But the moment she catches me by myself, she reverts to Mrs. Cleaning Machine.

"Scott is a real family-oriented sort of person, and he doesn't seem to mind his mom meddling in our affairs. But I say, 'This is our home, not hers, and she has no right coming in here and trying to take control.' When I complain, Scott gets mad and sulks on the couch. He doesn't understand why I don't appreciate his mom's help. Then I'm the one who feels like a dirty dog for griping. What in the world can I do?"

What indeed? What advice would you have given to Paula? We talked for over an hour, and basically, here's what I told her:

"First, it might help if you start thinking of your mother-in-law as a person who is on your team rather than merely on your case. Stop seeing her as your enemy and begin regarding her as a helping hand. In-laws don't come from outer space. They are normal people who need love, attention, and appreciation, just like the rest of us.

"Second, why not enlist her support? It sounds as though she has plenty of time and energy, so if she derives such pleasure from doing dishes, stack up a sinkful and have them waiting for her, while you use your time for something else. Let her do the jobs you don't enjoy and she does."

"Yes, but then she'll *really* think I'm a terrible house-keeper," Paula squealed in protest.

"So what? She probably thinks that now. But you know better. And if you tell Scott what you are doing, he won't be shocked if he gets home early some day and sees his mom doing dishes.

"You may want to invite her over on a specific workday to help you with the chores you're not thrilled about doing yourself. By asking her to come at a specific time, she may feel less inclined to simply 'pop over' so frequently.

"Most of all, it sounds to me as if your mother-in-law desperately needs to feel needed. You can help her feel important by listening when she gives advice. Don't reject her input simply because she's your mother-in-law. She may have some valuable ideas. Hang on to what is help-ful; let anything that hurts go in one ear and out the other. Think of her as an emotional cripple, and her critical com-ments as a little child's attempts to get attention.

"Be sure to thank her for any words of wisdom she shares with you—whether you can use them or not—and the work she helps you do. That way, she will feel appre-ciated and significant."

Admittedly, it wasn't the most profound advice I had ever offered, but it was practical, and Paula agreed to try it. About six weeks later, she stopped in to see me.

"You won't believe Scott's mom," she started.

"Wonder Woman?"

Paula laughed. "Yeah, but you know, she really can be a pretty nice woman. I tried what you said—remember? About leaving her a stack of dishes and all? I expressed to her how much I appreciated her help, and I told her if she wanted to plow into the stack of dishes in the sink, I'd set up the ironing board in the kitchen and do the ironing while she did the dishes. She loved the idea!

"She and I spent the next hour or so working together in the same room, talking, laughing, and honestly enjoying each other's company. She didn't think I was lazy anymore because she could clearly see that I was working right along with her. So we got the dishes and ironing done, and she did the dusting while I did the vacuuming. We became a pretty good team. When Scott came home, the house was spotless. His mom was happy, and I got my housework done with half the effort, which left me with more time and energy to spend the evening with Scott.

"The next day, Scott's mom called me up and asked me to go out to a restaurant for lunch. I think for the first time since Scott and I were married, she regards me as her son's wife. She's come to understand that I love her son as much as she does—I just don't love housework as much as she does! Still, we've become friends rather than foes, and that has certainly made life a lot more fun around our place. Scott has noticed, too, and he's real good about showing his love and appreciation to both his mom and to me.

"And guess what? Scott's mom doesn't come popping in on us anymore. She calls, and she and I make plans. Finally, I feel as if I'm in control of my own house.

"Isn't it funny? I didn't do anything all that different or difficult. I just started treating my mother-in-law as a person rather than a pest."

How to Get Along With Your In-Laws

What are some other things you can do that will help you to get *in*, or stay *in*, with your in-laws?

1. *Study your in-laws.* After all, these people have had a great impact upon the person you married; you might learn some significant things about your spouse, if you will take the time and effort to study his or her parents and siblings. Ask to see old family photographs, high school or college yearbooks, family wedding albums, or anything else that will provide clues to your spouse's background.

Ask your mate's parents about their family tree. Who were the first family members to come to this country? How did they get here; what did they do for a living? Listen carefully for hints that help you to understand the rationale and motives for their actions. You may never become best friends with your mate's family, but you might discover some common ground between you.

2. *Share your feelings about each other's family honestly but sensitively.* Remember, for better or for worse, your in-laws are still your partner's family members. When they rub you the wrong way, you needn't hide the fact from your spouse. Share your feelings honestly. The trick is to focus on your feelings, rather than on what you think that your in-law has done "wrong." Rather than saying, "Your parents are rude, ignorant snobs," you might try saying, "I feel as if your mom and dad are trying to avoid me."

Privacy is also important when discussing families. The best policy is this: Never criticize your in-laws to your partner. But if that promise is impossible or impractical for you to keep, at least hold yourself to this one: Keep it private! Never criticize your mate or any of your mate's family members in front of his or her parents, or yours. Wait until an opportunity arises when you and your partner can discuss the matter privately.

Keep in mind that the Bible instructs each of us to honor our parents. One of the Ten Commandments says, "Honor your father and your mother, that your days may be prolonged in the land which the Lord your God gives you" (Exodus 20:12). The Apostle Paul later pointed out that this is the first commandment that carries with it a promise: "That it may be well with you, and that you may live long on the earth" (Ephesians 6:3).

The word *honor* means "to show respect," "to treat one with kindness and dignity." Whether or not your parents or your in-laws live "respectable" lives, your obligation, according to the Bible, is to respect and honor them, if for no other reason than simply because they are your parents. This commandment has never been rescinded, nor will it be.

Consequently, when you criticize your partner's parents, not only are you being disrespectful but you are also making it extremely difficult for your mate to conform to the biblical pattern of honoring his or her mother and father. It's just not worth it to criticize your spouse's family. Rarely will anything constructive come from your critical comments.

Even if your partner makes negative remarks about his or her parents, don't you do it. Instead point out the positive; accentuate their strengths rather than their weaknesses. Encourage your spouse to honor his or her parents and you may be surprised when that response is reciprocated toward *your* parents.

3. *Show both of your families that you care about them.* The

key word here is *both*. What you do for one, you would be wise to do for the other. Equal treatment of the families is only fair. Most likely, one of the major fears on the part of your partner's parents and relatives when you and your mate got married was that you were going to steal away "the apple of their eye." You can calm those fears by assuring both families that you haven't abandoned them and that they still hold an important place in your lives.

The first time I visited Angela's relatives after we were engaged to be married, they all viewed me as though I were Attila the Hun, come to ravage the local virgin. I sensed their uneasiness about allowing their prize jewel to wander off into the foggy mist to the wilds of Pennsylvania, with a dark-haired, bearded, Arab sheik driving a black, 1978 Chrysler Cordoba, with black, Corinthian leather seats. Or maybe it was just my imagination.

Nevertheless, that night we all went to church together. The pastor recognized me and asked me to share a brief greeting and testimony. I was delighted to comply.

Every member of the family sat on the edge of his or her seat as the stranger from a far country began to speak. I shared briefly about my relationship with Jesus Christ, and then I told of my relationship with Angela. In closing, I asked for their prayers and I made them a promise. I said, "I've traveled over two million miles around the world and I had to come all the way to Marysville, Michigan, to find the woman God created just for me. But don't worry, I promise that after we are married, I will bring her back home to visit often."

Suddenly, I was the knight in shining armor. The barriers came tumbling down. You could almost hear the audience breathe a collective sigh of relief. Angela's family opened up their hearts and lovingly accepted me as part of them. Why? Because I made it clear that although our primary attachment was to each other, Angela and I had no intention of cutting ourselves off from our families.

You can do something similar by sending your parents an occasional greeting card, telephoning, remembering birthdays and anniversaries, and by visiting. Keep in mind the key word, though: *both*. If you live far from your families and telephone one set of parents frequently, you should phone the other set as well. If you buy a gift for one, buy for the other.

"That's silly!" some will say. Perhaps so, but if your goal is to get along with both sets of in-laws, it is wise to treat them equally. By doing so, you will remove or reduce a major source of parental competitiveness that has often created stumbling blocks for more than a few couples.

Holidays . . . Those Sticky Situations

In her book *Secrets of Staying in Love* (Nelson, 1984), Ruth Peale, wife of Norman Vincent Peale, shares an intimate account with which many Christian couples can identify:

> When we were first married, we always had to go to Mother Peale's home for Christmas. "I may not be here next year," she would say plaintively if I suggested going to my parents or making other plans. So we always wound up going there . . . and I always had to control and mask my resentment.

Sound familiar? Don't feel bad—almost everybody has relatives who "probably won't be here next year, so we'd better spend this last holiday with them." Amazing, isn't it, the longevity of some of those dear ones?

Understand, we need to be sensitive to the needs of our soon-to-be-gone loved ones, whether *gone* means death or merely moving to a far-off or less accessible location. But it is unfair to stick your spouse's head (or yours!) in a guillotine of guilt. Don't do it, and don't allow other people to do it to you.

So how does one resolve those sticky holiday situations, especially Thanksgiving and Christmas? Some couples try to keep everybody happy by putting in an appearance at both parents' meal tables. Before I was married, I watched with amused interest as my brothers attempted that bulging balancing act.

For several years in succession, my brothers and their wives ate Thanksgiving or Christmas dinner with our family, then drove to the homes of their wives' parents and pretended they were famished in the face of another feast.

"Mmm-mm. Turkey and stuffing! My favorite. Haven't had a meal like this in . . . at least fifteen minutes!" Holidays meant one thing for my brothers and their wives: Pepto-Bismol.

After a few years of this gluttonous gobbling, my mother and dad proposed a compromise: "Let's have Thanksgiving or Christmas *breakfast* here, then you guys can go to your in-laws later in the day for dinner." It made sense—unless you happen to know my mother.

When my mom cooks a holiday breakfast, you could feed the entire Fourth Infantry. I've seen big-time hotel buffets that don't have a breakfast spread like my mother's. She gives you the works: eggs, pancakes, sausage, bacon, cereal, juices, toast, cinnamon rolls, waffles. If you can imagine it for breakfast, she'll prepare it.

Still, my brothers and their wives were a bit happier; at least they got a break between "pigging out" for breakfast and stuffing themselves at dinner. Both brothers began to resemble the Goodyear Blimp, but the in-laws were happy.

For several years, I watched this spectacle of holiday table hopping with bemused objectivity and pity. Then Angela and I got married. Now it is no longer mere table hopping—we engage in serious *state* hopping. We have Christmas breakfast in Pennsylvania with my family and Christmas dinner in Michigan with Angela's family. We feel fortunate, though; we have an entire turnpike between our breakfast and dinner tables.

We have also tried a variety of combinations in our attempts to be fair to both families. We've spent holidays at home and invited everyone to our home. We've spent Thanksgiving with one family and Christmas with the other.

What's the solution to such holiday hassles? Equality. Angela and I are travel addicts. We don't really mind driving five hundred miles in a day in order to spend the holiday with both of our families. For most people, however, equality will mean Thanksgiving with one set of parents, Christmas with the other; or perhaps alternating years, visiting one family one year and the other family the following year.

Whatever you do, don't allow those blessed, special times of the year to be destroyed by disagreements over where you will spend the holiday. Two principles are important in this regard: *Consider creative alternatives* and *seek to compromise*. Rather than fighting over family functions, look for alternative means of satisfying both sets of in-laws. Perhaps you might ask both of your families to get together at your place, or ask one family to invite the other, so you can celebrate together. Compromise is the key. Stay flexible and seek harmony and unity among your family members.

United We Stand

Another suggestion for getting along with your in-laws is this: *Demonstrate that you and your mate are indivisible.* Show your family, friends, and everyone else that you and your marriage partner are a couple. You are committed to each other. Undivided. One.

How can you do this? First, you must present a united front. Don't allow your parents or relatives to "run down" your partner behind his or her back, and don't *you* be a party to such. You must make it clear that, after the Lord, your mate comes first in your life. When somebody is berating your spouse, he or she is berating you. Don't let anyone drive a wedge of discontent between you and your mate.

Don't reveal marital confidences that you know your mate would not appreciate having discussed outside your home. For example, even in this current age of openness, most married couples prefer to keep mum about matters pertaining to their sex lives, marital stress, financial status, certain issues relating to their children, and sometimes even religious topics. Rarely does good result from talking about private matters with people other than your spouse, unless you are in a counseling situation.

If something is a secret between you and your spouse,

do not betray that confidence. Don't tell your brother, your sister, your mother, father, or best friend. Build trust into your relationship by making it a habit not to discuss with anyone other than your partner confidential information that you and your mate regard as private.

A second way you can model your unity as a couple is to spell out clearly what type of relationship you want to have with your relatives. If you enjoy people dropping in spontaneously and unannounced, fine. Tell your family and friends. If, however, you want to guard your privacy, don't spout such silly tripe as "Drop over anytime. We're always glad to see you!" Besides being a lie (nobody is *always* happy to have company!), you are sending a misleading message. You'd be better off to invite specific people over at a designated time. That way, they will get the idea that you schedule your social life, that you relish your relationship with your husband or wife, and you may not wish to relinquish your private time together on a moment's notice.

As an overriding principle, keep in mind that when you and your partner married, you committed yourselves to leaving father and mother, cleaving to each other, and becoming one flesh (Genesis 2:24). That is the biblical pattern for marriage, and it should be the goal of every married couple. Leaving your parents and cleaving to your mate means a lot more than merely living with another person. Leaving also includes psychological separation—cutting the apron strings. When you marry, you are no longer attached to Mom and Dad in quite the same way; your primary allegiance is now to your partner.

Practically, that means when there is a choice whether you will attempt to please your parents or please your partner, the priority goes to your partner. Your parents and in-laws may offer valuable suggestions about many aspects of your marriage, and you should listen carefully and consider their input. But if your marriage is to succeed as the "one flesh" unit God brought together for His purposes, you must make your decisions based upon what will glorify Him and what will be good for you and your mate.

What Is the Proper Parental Role?

Believe it or not, your parents and in-laws *can* be a great blessing to your marriage. Don't be deceived by society's sick caricatures. Author Gary Chapman contends in his book *Toward a Growing Marriage* (Moody, 1979), "In our society, mother-in-law jokes have become so rampant that many people feel ashamed to admit they have a good relationship with their mother-in-law. The truth is that a godly mother-in-law is a treasure second only to a godly husband or wife." The same could be said about a good, godly father-in-law.

Currently, more jokes and horror stories are circulated about meddlesome mothers-in-law than about fussy fathers-in-law, but don't be surprised if you see that changing in the years ahead. Until recent years, mothers have been more intimately involved in the raising of the children—no wonder then the strained, painful experience when Mom feels her role has been superseded.

Two factors combine to set up an interesting scenario for the not-so-distant future. Because more women are entering the work force, thus spending less time with their children, their influence is lessened. At the same time, due to a renewed emphasis upon modern-day fathers bearing more responsibility in the child-rearing process, we may soon be hearing more stories of fatherly interference. I doubt that mother-in-law mayhem will ever disappear entirely. Maybe the matriarchal instincts that most women seem to possess make it impossible for fathers-in-law to ever provoke the sort of friction generated by mothers-in-law.

Still, it is possible to enjoy a rich relationship with both your parents and your in-laws if everyone will understand the rules and the roles. Simply put, the rule is that once you are married, your parents move into an advisory role. They have a wealth of wisdom, counsel, suggestions, and prayer support that they can share with you. Don't be so stubborn that you automatically discard their ideas as interference. They may be right!

Jeff writes off Carla's dad, Joe, as a whining, griping grouch. "He's always telling me how to take care of my lawn; I ought to fertilize that part, plant shrubs over there, water at night instead of in the morning," Jeff groused. "I wish Joe would go water his own garden and let me alone." In fact, Joe is an expert landscaper and a virtual walking encyclopedia of horticultural knowledge. His approach to his son-in-law could certainly be improved, but his information could also keep his grandkids playing on green grass instead of brown dirt.

The advantage of having in-laws is that you have a new and exciting opportunity to develop fresh family relationships—only this time, you can make them better. For example, if your past includes painful childhood memories, you now have a second chance to enjoy a relationship with an older adult, without the hurt. Similarly, your in-laws may become the parent or sibling you never had.

Bob enjoys being able to discuss deep, theological, biblical issues with Roy, his father-in-law. Bob's own father was not a Christian and had no interest in spiritual subjects, but Bob is now making up for lost time. Cindy looks forward to her weekly tennis games with her father-in-law. As she was growing up, Cindy's dad was consumed with making a living for the family; he had little time for tennis, and even less energy. Cindy now enjoys a relationship with her father-in-law that she never experienced with her own dad.

Certainly, nobody will ever *replace* your mom and dad, but a godly set of in-laws may be the next-best thing.

The "disadvantage" of having in-laws is that just about the time you finally resolve most of your emotional conflicts stemming from past experiences with your own parents, you marry someone and inherit another set of parents to raise. God sure has a great sense of humor!

5
How to Fight as Christians

Marriage Myth Number Four:
Christian couples rarely disagree, argue, or fight. Or, "We can solve all of our disputes through straight, honest communication."

"Never go to bed mad. Stay up and fight."
                                        Phyllis Diller

● ● ● ● ● ● ● ● ● ● ● ● ● ●

"That's it! I've had it. I'm leaving!" Patrick shouted, as he slammed the bedroom door behind him.

"Well, good!" Vicki retorted, "and don't let the door hit you on your way out. On second thought . . . let it hit you!"

The newly married couple was having their first spat as husband and wife. It had started over something silly, but the argument continued to escalate until both Patrick and Vicki were hurling insults back and forth. Finally, in exasperation, Patrick threw up his hands and began packing his bags.

"I'm going!" he called to Vicki, a bit reluctantly, as he pushed open the screen door with his suitcase and shuffled onto the front porch.

How to Fight as Christians

"Good! Go on and go, 'cause I'm going, too!" Vicki yelled.

Patrick heaved his suitcase into the backseat of his car, slammed the door, and slumped behind the wheel. He punched the gas pedal down hard, and in a flash, the car roared out of the driveway.

Suddenly, a painful thought struck him: "I don't have anyplace to go!" he said aloud. Most of Patrick's relatives lived hundreds of miles away, and unless he wanted to quit his job, he still had to be at work on Monday morning.

I've got an idea, Patrick thought. *I'll go to Vicki's mother and dad's place. They like me. They will allow me to stay there.* Patrick pointed the car in the direction of Vicki's parents' home.

The young husband had no sooner arrived at his in-laws' place and had barely begun to explain his plight before another car screeched into the driveway. Patrick could tell by the sound of the door slamming that it was Vicki's car. He and Vicki's parents ran outside onto the porch.

"What are you doing here?" Vicki screamed when she saw her husband.

"I didn't have anyplace to go," Patrick replied almost apologetically. "What are *you* doing here?"

"I didn't have anywhere else to go, either," Vicki admitted, her voice cracking and tears starting to trickle down her cheeks.

"Well, you can't stay here. *I* came here," Patrick snarled.

"What do you mean, I can't stay here? These are *my* parents and this is their home!"

"Oh, yeah? Don't you remember what you used to say *before* we were married—that your parents would be *my* parents, too? So here I am at Mom and Dad's."

"That's ridiculous. They're *my* parents."

"And mine."

"But you left first!"

"That's right. I did, so I should get first bid on staying with Mom and Dad."

Slowly but surely, Patrick and Vicki began to realize the absurdity of their conversation.

"This is stupid. Why don't we just go home?" Patrick suggested, his arms open wide.

Vicki fell into Patrick's arms and began bawling. "I'm sorry. I'm sorry. I didn't mean all those horrible things I said."

"No, no. I'm the one who is sorry. I was a big dummy," Patrick answered. "Let's go home."

He and Vicki tumbled into Patrick's car and headed for home. "Thanks for all your help, folks," Patrick called out the window as he waved good-bye.

Vicki's parents stood on the porch, chuckling. They hadn't said a word throughout the entire encounter. The couple shook their heads, shrugged their shoulders, and returned, arm in arm, to the solace of their living room.

"Kids," drawled Vicki's mom. "I wish they'd learn how to fight right."

The truth is, most Christians don't know how to have a good fight. Christian couples can and do experience serious conflicts within their marriages. But to fight like Christians? Ah . . . that's another story.

My mom and dad didn't believe in "agreeing to disagree" or "disagreeing in love." To them, it was, "All's fair in love and war," which left open any option short of mauling or murder, and I'm sure they considered those. To this day, after more than forty years of marriage, one of them will quip, "We never once thought of divorce; murder, maybe—but divorce, never!"

Still, some of their verbal bouts entertained the entire neighborhood. Usually, the battle raged for several days before Mom would seek sanctuary in her parents' home— four hours away in Niagara Falls, New York.

Dad often used these periods of Mom's absence to display his wonderful but slightly wacky sense of humor. One of his specialties was to start a rumor among Mom's "good church friends," and then sit back and watch to see how far they would spread it.

Once, while Mom was planning her counterattack in Niagara Falls, accompanied by my brother, one of the congregational busybodies asked about Mom not being in church. Dad immediately saw his chance.

"I don't know," he countered. "She didn't tell me anything; she just left."

"No!" cried the Church Gossip.

"Yeah, we split everything down the middle—she took half and I took half. She took one kid and I took the other. She took half the table, and I took the other. She took one-half of the bed, and I took the other."

"No! I don't believe it!" lied the busybody.

"Yes, it's sad, isn't it?" Dad was struggling to keep a straight face, but the busybody was buying his outlandish tale, so he continued to stretch it. "We sawed the couch in two so she could have her half and I could have mine. We did the same with the piano."

"Oh, how terrible!" The Church Gossip gasped as she strutted off in a huff.

"Yep, sure is," said Dad with a knowing smile on his face as he watched her hurry away.

Within days, the news had spread all over town that the Abrahams had separated and would soon be finalizing their divorce. Imagine the confusion when Mom showed up in church the following Sunday—sitting with Dad and the family!

After the service, the Church Gossip caught Mom on her way out the door. "Oh, Mrs. Abraham, I am so sorry to hear about you and your husband," the woman whispered.

Mom looked at Dad and scowled. She had no idea what he had said, but she knew he had been up to something. She decided to play along and answered, "Thank you very much. I'm sure everything will work out just fine."

I think that was one of those occasions when murder might have crossed Mom's mind.

Of course Christian couples have conflicts. My mom and dad did; so will you and your partner at some point. Every intimate relationship includes struggle, and Christians are not immune. Marriage does not alleviate conflicts; it creates them! As a Christian, though, you can take advantage of a problem-solving resource that an unbelieving couple does not share: the supernatural power of Christ.

How can you do that? Let's look at some do's and don'ts of fighting as Christians.

The Rules of the Ring

Here are some strategies you and your spouse can use to stop minor skirmishes before they mushroom into major blowups.

1. *DON'T go to bed mad.* The Apostle Paul may not com-

pletely agree with Phyllis Diller's advice to "stay up and fight," but in Ephesians 4:26, 27 he does provide an extremely practical principle: "Do not let the sun go down on your anger, and do not give the devil an opportunity."

In other words, "Don't go to bed mad." You may have to stay up awfully late at times, but better to do that than to allow problems to enlarge overnight, giving the devil an opportunity to destroy your relationship.

Don't go to bed mad, but do go to bed together. When Bill and Debbie have a fight, he stays up and watches television until the wee hours of the morning, rather than sleeping in the same bed as his wife.

"I'll be along in a few minutes," he says. Hours later, when Debbie is sleeping, Bill slides quietly into their bed, carefully avoiding any contact with his wife. Consequently, they become even further alienated from each other.

Don't allow such a destructive habit to develop in your marriage. Go to bed *together*. Establish some ritual between the two of you that puts a lid on the day, whether or not you have had a conflict. A hug, a kiss, a loving touch, expressions of sexual intimacy, a prayer together, anything that says in a positive way, "Good night, my love," will remind you that the two of you are still connected and your marriage pact remains intact.

As part of his prescription for a superb marriage, Dr. Ed Wheat, author of *Love Life for Every Married Couple* (Zondervan, 1980), instructs couples as follows:

> Try to go to bed when your partner does *every* night.
> Have a period of fifteen to thirty minutes every night
> to lie in each other's arms in the dark before you

drift off to sleep. Whisper together, sharing private thoughts and pleasant little experiences of the day. Avoid controversial or negative topics. This is the time to build intimacy and wind down for sleep. You will become used to sharing things with each other that you would not otherwise mention. In each other's arms the hurts and frustrations of the day are healed. You may want to pray together at this time, or just relax in the comfort of physically felt love.

2. *DON'T expect immediate solutions to every problem.* Most minor conflicts can be quickly and easily resolved, but "the biggies" might require more time. That's okay. You don't have to solve every issue before going to bed, but you don't have to let the crisis continue to bug you all night long, either. Let it go. Agree to come back to it another time. Plan a definite appointment with each other to discuss the problem, pray together, and then say, "Good night." You may be pleasantly surprised to discover that the problem doesn't seem nearly as large in the light of a new day.

Certain times are more conducive to arguments than others. When you or your spouse comes home after a long, hard, exasperating day at work, that is definitely not the time to discuss disagreeable topics. The saying "Timing is everything" is never more appropriate than it is when applied to marital conflicts.

Ruth Bell Graham, wife of world-famous evangelist Billy Graham, offers a suggestion for knowing when not to disagree: "For one thing, it is not wise to disagree with a man when he is tired, hungry, worried, ill, preoccupied, or pressured" (*It's My Turn,* Revell, 1982).

Be brave enough to say, "Honey, this isn't the best time for this discussion," or "Let's talk about this after the kids are in bed," or "Please wait until we get home and we will talk about this in private." Then do it. It is an extremely unwise husband or wife who forces the issue onto the table when the timing isn't right.

3. *DO let little things pass, but DON'T let them build*. Not everything is worth getting all hyped up about, so choose your battle lines carefully. Ask yourself, *Is this really important? Does this matter enough to merit a confrontation?*

In his excellent book *Seeds of Greatness* (Revell, 1983), Denis Waitley points out that failure to make wise choices in the area of anger and conflict may be more costly than you think. Dr. Waitley explains:

> There is a psychological myth that venting your anger is the healthy thing to do. The problem with venting anger is that you can't take back what you said or did to the person receiving it. . . . Ask any wife or mother who has been a victim of a husband's or a child's tantrums. . . .
>
> All of us have a "stress" savings account deposited in our bodies as our life-force. The object is to spend it wisely over the longest time span possible. The difference between our "stress" savings account and a normal bank account is that we cannot make any more deposits into the "stress" account. We can only make withdrawals. The reason most people age at such different rates is that our society is full of "big spenders" who overreact to harmless circumstances as if they were life-or-death matters. We see it every day on our freeways on the way to work. . . .

It is better to learn to adapt to and live with situations than to react in a state of alarm and resistance. Alarm and resistance as a life-style lead to early exhaustion. Emotionally upset individuals literally withdraw all of their energy reserves ahead of schedule and run out of life too soon.

Simply put, don't sweat the small stuff! Let the little things go. But, at the same time, be careful not to allow them to build up. Remember, if you accumulate enough of those little things without ever addressing them or letting off a little steam, it's as if you continue to pump hot air into a balloon. It can only stretch so far before it explodes.

Aunt Mabel should have gone to prison at age seventy-seven, but the judge was lenient because of her age. Her crime? She killed her husband, Harold, by hitting him over the head with a frying pan.

Throughout their marriage, Harold treated Mabel horribly. He incessantly insulted her, made fun of her, and regarded her as a servant for his convenience. Despite such awful treatment, Mabel remained loyal to Harold for more than fifty years.

One day Mabel was complaining to a neighbor about Harold's constant harassment. The neighbor innocuously answered, "Why, Mabel, if my husband ever said anything like that to me, I'd take the heaviest frying pan I have, and while he was sleeping at night, I'd whack him over the head with it!"

The neighbor's idea piqued Mabel's interest. A few days later, Harold was at his ornery worst. All evening he continued to hurl abuse at Mabel, nitpicking about anything: "The supper is cold"; "the house is a mess"; "this room is too hot." Each bit of his harangue stretched Mabel's patience a little further beyond her limits.

The final blow came when Harold deliberately changed the channel on the television while Mabel was watching her favorite program. Mabel's blood began to boil.

"Harold, I am *going* to watch my story," Mabel said defiantly.

"Oh, yeah? Over my dead body!"

Harold shouldn't have said that.

Later that night, as soon as Harold began to snore, Mabel slipped into the kitchen, found the heaviest frying pan in the cupboard, and bashed in Harold's head. When she went to trial, the judge could not believe that the sweet, little septuagenarian could possibly have been in her right mind when she split Harold's skull, so he ruled that she was too old and mentally incompetent to stand trial.

Mabel happily continued to watch whatever she wanted on television until she passed away at ninety-five years of age!

Did Mabel kill Harold over a television program? Of course not. But it was one little thing, built upon another, until she couldn't take it any longer. Don't sweat the small stuff, but don't let the small stuff make you sweat, either. Confront your mate when and where it really matters.

4. *DO stick to the issue.* If you are angry because your husband spent the entire afternoon watching a football game and failed to take out the garbage, speak to that issue specifically. Don't drag every stray deficiency in his character into the discussion.

Similarly, if you are upset because your wife was a bit

flirtatious with your best friend, stick to that point and deal with it, but don't dredge up data on every guy she ever dated before marrying you.

Generalizations such as "You never take out the garbage!" or "You are always such a flirt!" will not help to resolve a conflict. When you use words such as *always* and *never*, you are rolling an insurmountable obstacle into the path of any real communication.

Make a conscious effort to avoid comments such as these:

"You never help around the house."

"You always spend more money than you should."

"Why don't you just stop and ask for directions? We've already gone around this block fourteen times. You are always so stubborn!"

Rather than generalizing, focus on one matter at a time. If you stick to the issue at hand and deal with it in a sincere, straightforward manner, you may be surprised to discover that many conflicts can be resolved in a matter of minutes.

5. *DON'T blame; DO emphasize what you feel.* Assessing blame rarely brings positive results in a relationship. Our society is obsessed with seeking a scapegoat to blame for our maladies, but blame only causes deeper division; it forces the other person to become defensive. Furthermore, in most marital spats, neither party is without fault. Trying to figure out who is to blame is a waste of time and energy. If you are going into the ring with your spouse hoping for a knockout, you had better examine your motives. In your marriage, when one partner wins at the expense of the other, you both lose. Remember the old

saying, "You don't win an *argument*; you can only win an *agreement*."

Avoid blame, but do concentrate on expressing your feelings. Rather than blasting your partner for his or her behavior, it is always wiser to emphasize what *you* are feeling inside. For example, instead of complaining to your husband that he is spending too much time at the golf course, say, "I know you love to play golf, and I'm glad you enjoy it, but I feel as if I'm not as important to you as your golf game." Now, your assessment of the situation may be absolutely correct, but you haven't put your partner down by saying it.

One word of caution when speaking about feelings: It is foolish to criticize your spouse for feeling the way he or she does. To say "You shouldn't feel that way" is useless. If your partner expresses honest feelings of anger, acknowledge them as real. Whether or not you understand or agree with the feelings is irrelevant. What matters is that you make your mate aware that *you* regard those feelings as important enough to talk about. You can say, "Honey, I honestly didn't realize how upset you felt, but now that I do, let's talk about it." Or, "I understand that you are angry, but I'm not sure I understand *why* you are so mad. Tell me why you feel that way."

6. *DO keep it clean; DON'T use a club!* Perhaps one of the most important principles in solving marriage conflicts, and yet one of the most frequently ignored, is the Apostle Paul's admonition that you get into the habit of "speaking the truth in love" (Ephesians 4:15). Certainly, if something is bothering you about your marriage, you need to get it out in the open. Neither you nor your partner will profit by tamping repressed feelings down deeper into your sub-

conscious mind, or by allowing problems to smolder beneath the surface of your relationship.

Nevertheless, consider this: Not everything that is true needs to be spoken. Harsh words hurt, whether or not they are true, when they are spoken in truth but not in love. Your goal should be to speak the truth in love, to strengthen your marriage, to build your partner up, not to tear each other down. Strive to keep your spat on a positive track, if possible. You can often do this by asking yourself the simple question, *Do I want to hurt my marriage partner, or do I want to solve this problem?* Obviously, if you are trying to hurt the person to whom you are married, you have bigger problems than the one immediately at hand.

If you are going to fight like Christians, make the rule, "No clubs allowed." The Bible says, "Be angry, and yet do not sin" (Ephesians 4:26). When you resort to clubbing your partner, verbally or physically, you can be sure that your anger has crossed the line and developed into sin. Chuck Swindoll commented upon this scriptural truth in *Strike the Original Match*:

> All of us know in our consciences when anger has become sin. . . . Bursts of temper are sinful. Anger that slips out of control is sinful. Anger that plans to hurt another member of the family or another individual is sinful anger. Anger that is expressed in profanity is, too. You know the point where your anger becomes sin. . . . When we attack the person rather than the problem, we move into deadly areas. When we make things personal or assault motives rather than dealing with the wrong *situation*, we're treading

on thin ice. When we reject rather than reprove, it's harmful.

Certainly, no couple should ever resort to physical violence to resolve a conflict. Pushing, shoving, punching, or kicking your partner are serious offenses and should not be permitted. If such expressions of anger exist in your relationship, I urge you to seek professional help immediately.

For many marriage partners, verbal abuse is almost as painful. When you indulge in backstabbing, name-calling, threats, sexual slurs, or sarcastic remarks, you are picking up a club and beating your partner. Sometimes the blows can be deadly to your relationship.

Remember, your negative words have a longer half-life than radioactive waste. Words have an existence all their own. Once you have said them, you can never "unsay" them. Oh, sure, you can say, "I take it back," but that's impossible.

Sometimes in the heat of battle, a marriage partner says things he or she might not mean. Unfortunately, that does not negate the power of such statements to sear into the heart and mind of the other person. Often, even after forgiveness is sought and granted, those memories survive.

"I hate you!" Betty screamed at Sam. "I never loved you in the first place. I don't know why I ever married you!" Betty later apologized to her husband and Sam forgave her . . . but he has never forgotten those words. Although he chooses to forgive and he refuses to allow himself to dwell on the past, every once in a while, when things aren't going quite right between Betty and him, those words come back to haunt him.

Again, the Apostle Paul points out the best formula for keeping your conduct clean, even in the midst of marital conflicts: "Let all bitterness and wrath and anger and clamor and slander be put away from you, along with all malice. And be kind to one another, tender-hearted, forgiving each other, just as God in Christ also has forgiven you" (Ephesians 4:31, 32).

Notice Paul's emphasis upon forgiveness. This is not merely advice for mopping up a marital mess. To forgive each other as Jesus Christ has forgiven you is a foundational principle for successful Christian relationships.

What About When You Can't Agree?

Inevitably, in every marriage, an issue arises upon which loving partners cannot come to an amicable agreement. What should you do then?

First, call a truce. If you are spinning your wheels, nothing is to be gained by more intense friction. Sure, you may generate more heat, but the ice you are slipping on may already be far too thin for safety. Don't push it. If you can't resolve the conflict, at least reassure each other of your love. Saying something as simple as "I may be mad at you about this, but I still love you" will provide the needed reassurance.

Second, keep the lines of communication open. Don't slam any doors behind you, figuratively or literally. *Listen.* Maybe you are not really hearing what your mate is saying. Ask your partner to repeat his or her position. Request that your spouse review your position. Often, what your partner heard you say is not what you said or not what you meant to say.

Third, be sure to saturate your situation with enough time and prayer. If possible, allow the problem to wait before making a final decision. Perhaps the Lord will bless you with more information, keener insight, or greater objectivity, any or all of which will help you in the decision-making process. Extremely few issues in marriage demand a crisis-type, immediate decision. Take time to pray about the problem. Take time to talk through it.

Kevin Leman, popular psychologist and best-selling author, passed on to me an invaluable piece of advice that James Dobson gave to him: "Anytime you have a major decision to make, take time to run it by your wife." Taking any action that affects your marriage without taking the time to talk and pray through it with your partner is almost always counterproductive.

When those rare occasions arise in which a decision must be made immediately, and you and your partner cannot agree, I believe that the husband, as the spiritual head of the household, must do what he feels is best for the family, taking full responsibility for that decision. This is not a chauvinistic statement, merely a matter of order and function.

To Love, Honor, and . . . Negotiate?

For most couples, fighting is no fun. Granted, marital conflicts can be productive and may actually work to strengthen your relationship, but if you are like most people, you probably prefer a more harmonious homelife.

Don't be deceived by all the talk-show advisers, spouting the latest "psychobabble," advocating the value of venting your anger at your spouse. Since the 1960s, more and more secular psychologists have been touting the merits of "letting it all hang out" in the marriage relationship, openly expressing everything and anything you happen to feel. In recent years, this view has invaded Christian circles. Nowadays, a plethora of Christian counselors, authors, and ministers is applauding marriage partners who hold nothing back; couples are encouraged to fight it out.

I disagree. While I am not advocating that you conceal the truth from your spouse or repress feelings that need to be expressed, I believe we need to rediscover the virtues of avoiding conflict whenever possible (*see* Romans 12:17–21). After thirty years of marital *glasnost*, our divorce rate has not gone down but up; spousal abuse is growing more commonplace; more couples than ever are expressing displeasure in their relationships. A vast number of marriage partners are merely coexisting.

I'm not the only one questioning the value of dropping emotional bombshells on your mate. In their book *Husbands and Wives*, noted psychologists Melvin Kinder and Connell Cowan decry the notion that we have endured for the past three decades—that the more open you are with your mate, the more satisfying your marriage—as downright drivel:

> This is a belief that is so pervasive it is taken as gospel by the vast majority of couples in America. It would be nice if it were true, but it's not. Relationships are not so simple that mere openness, the expression of what we think and feel, will instantly produce close-

ness. Like so many other myths that confuse marriage today, the idea that openness is synonymous with intimacy and is therefore a prerequisite for a good marriage may have caused as much harm as good.

Sure, partners fight, even in the best of marriages; some couples become rather adept at marital sparring; some even enjoy it as a method of releasing tensions. But the truth is that not everyone handles marriage conflict well, and while it sounds fine to say, "If we're going to fight, let's fight fairly," few couples actually do. Often, fighting brings out the bully in a person, one partner attempting to bolster his or her self-esteem at the expense of the other. Some people threaten violence or divorce. Others simply try to outwit or outmanipulate their partners. Perhaps, as fallen sinners, most of us are simply too selfish to fight fairly.

That's why I prefer Paul's prescription:

> Let no unwholesome word proceed from your mouth, but only such a word as is good for edification according to the need of the moment, that it may give grace to those who hear. And do not grieve the Holy Spirit of God, by whom you were sealed for the day of redemption.
>
> Ephesians 4:29, 30

How to Avoid a Fight

Myriad marital conflicts could be avoided by incorporating three simple words: *I was wrong.* Say them aloud one time. Go ahead. It won't hurt. "I was wrong." Unfamiliar, huh?

Here are three more words that could save you thousands of others: *You are right*. It's tough to start a fight or to keep one going when either one of the above sentences is spoken.

If you are wrong, admit it! Why rip apart your marriage for the sake of stubbornness and pride? Surrender! Concede graciously, but concede.

A few other words that come in handy around the house are *I'm sorry*, *Please forgive me*, and *I forgive you*. Try them. You'll be amazed at how they can cause marital tensions to melt.

6
Just Like Mom and Dad

Marriage Myth Number Five:
Real men don't wash dishes, and real women don't wash cars. Or, "Our marriage will stick with the stereotypes established by our parents."

"Some men expect their wives to dress like a peacock, sing like a nightingale, act like a lovebird . . . and work like a horse!"

"How can you tell who is in charge in this marriage? When you get up in the middle of the night to turn out the light, stop; turn around, look back to see who is in bed. *That's* who is in charge!"

Gallagher

"Let us now set forth one of the fundamental truths about marriage: the wife is in charge. Or, to put it another way, the husband is not."

Bill Cosby

● ● ● ● ● ● ● ● ● ● ● ● ● ● ●

I grew up with "the Beaver," as in "Leave It to Beaver." Maybe you did, too. Every week (and eventually, every afternoon as the show went into reruns), I watched while Mr. and Mrs. Cleaver guided Wally and "the Beav" through a maze of problems, often complicated by Eddie Haskell but always solved before the show concluded. It was a nice formula. Wally or Beaver got in a mess and came home to Mrs. Cleaver, who encouraged the boys to do their homework and wash up for supper. Mrs. Cleaver *always* had a super supper ready to be enjoyed the moment Mr. Cleaver came home from work. Somewhere in the midst of one of those delicious dinners, somebody spilled the beans and let it be known to Mr. Cleaver that one of the guys had a problem.

Mr. Cleaver, in his infinite wisdom, could solve almost any dilemma. Had VCRs been invented, he probably could have set the timer. To me, Willie Mays meant the best in baseball, Billy Graham was the world's greatest preacher, and Ward Cleaver epitomized what it meant to be a husband and father.

By the time I married, a strange phenomenon had taken place in society. Ward Cleaver had been replaced by Mr. Mom; men's and women's roles had undergone a major metamorphosis; the rules had changed and I found myself feeling weird. Here's why: Although I am a late-twentieth-century, modern-day, progressive sort of guy who believes in helping with the housework and other traditionally "female" chores, I grew up in the 1950s and 1960s, when a different set of ideals and roles were expected of, and modeled by, husbands and wives all around me.

A simple example: At family gatherings, nobody thought twice about having a giant meal, after which the guys would retreat to the TV room to watch the football game while the women cleared the table and did the dishes. If one of the men had volunteered to help with the cleanup chores, he would have been ostracized, branded a traitor, and shot at sunrise. Although nobody said so, the message was implied, "Real men don't do dishes." (Nor did real men change diapers.)

When Angela and I married, it wasn't the revolution in sexual roles and attitudes but stark economic realities that turned us into a two-career couple. We both had to work to survive financially. I knew my wife worked hard as a dental hygienist. Consequently, I was always glad to help with our household chores. Beyond that, I felt it was only fair for me to share the burden of housework.

Still, I had difficulty shedding the attitudes and roles with which I had grown accustomed and comfortable. Mom and Dad's values reverberated through my mind. My mom worked, yet she seemed to manage. She always had the meals ready, the clothes ironed, and the house clean enough to keep the board of health from sending us to jail. And she was happy without Dad doing dishes, running the vacuum cleaner, or pairing socks. *Why couldn't Angela and I just do things the same way they did?* I thought.

On the other hand, Angela had spent a large sum of money securing her education, part of which had convinced her that if the woman is going to help bring home the bacon, the man should help fry it. Her problem, however, was similar to mine. She had grown up in a large Italian family, an environment in which a woman's role was to have babies, fatten them up with pasta, and take care of any other needs they might have for the rest of their lives.

Even though she worked an eight-to-five job, Angela began to feel guilty for not taking full responsibility for her home. Meanwhile, despite my willingness to help with domestic chores and my appreciation for Angela's dilemma, I began to feel cheated because Angela wasn't able to maintain her career and still do all the things my mom did for me as I was growing up.

Before we were married, we had assumed that both Angela and I would be working outside the home, at least until we had children. We had discussed our jobs, the amounts of money we needed, our goals, and a host of other issues pertaining to daily life together. The one issue we hardly discussed was *daily life together!*

Now, as a married couple, the issues we faced were not the traditional questions of "provider versus homemaker" but much more nitty-gritty questions such as these:

Who should scrub the bathtub?

Who takes out the garbage?

Who goes grocery shopping?

Who changes the toilet paper roll when it is empty? (If you say, "Obviously, the person who used it last," you probably have not been married very long.)

Who waits for the cable TV repairperson?

Who shovels the snow off the car on a cold winter morning?

Who cuts the grass?

Who does the dishes?

Who makes the bed?

And perhaps the most delicate question of marriage, "Who is going to clean the commode?"

Many modern-day married couples are experiencing something similar. You probably didn't get married for the purpose of keeping track of somebody else's socks or car keys, but by now, either you or your partner probably is. As one sly sage observed, "Marriage is still the most expensive way to get your laundry done for free. But nowadays, the big question is, 'Who is going to *do* the laundry?' "

Me Tarzan, You . . . Jack?

Confusion over responsibilities in marriage is nothing new; confusion over *roles* in marriage is an issue that has only recently surged onto the scene. Traditionally, Dad was the hardworking provider, going to work each day and returning to his fawning family, well tended by an adoring wife and mother. Currently, for various reasons, many wives are no longer content to merely cook, clean, and take care of the children, and they are entering the work force outside the home. As a result, husbands and dads are discovering that their roles are rapidly being re-defined, almost by default.

The old tags are being torn asunder. For example, if you want to create a stir or get in a fight at a party, just start a conversation about "women's work" in the home or "the husband's role."

Admittedly, discussions of modern-day husband-and-wife responsibilities raise many previously unaddressed or inadequately addressed questions. For example, how does a contemporary couple reconcile roles of indepen-dence and freedom for each partner with commitment, mutual dependence, and biblical patterns of headship and submission?

Unfortunately, much of the current confusion in many marriages is the result of misguided misinterpretations of male headship and female submission inherited from past generations. Rick and Cindy are suffering through such a situation.

Rick grew up in a Christian family where his dad was "head of the house." Sadly, in Rick's family, that meant male dominance and female submission; male privilege and female provision. Rick's dad had the attitude, "Basically, I do what I want and my wife and family are here to help and support me. We go where I want and spend money to promote, achieve, or acquire my interests. This family's decisions are made on the basis of how they will impact upon me."

Of course, Rick's dad never *said* those things. After all, he was a "Christian." He wouldn't think of saying anything so selfish. He simply lived that way. He assumed that rights, privileges, and servitude were inherently his fringe benefits for being husband and father. His family owed him respect and service because he was the "head" of the home.

And guess who has dragged those same warped attitudes of male headship into his marriage? Too bad; Rick has grown up to be "just like Dad," and Cindy is living with a fellow who wants to run his family exactly "the way Dad did."

Cindy, however, refuses to become a doormat. Whenever Rick goes into his headship routine, Cindy's pride perks up and she responds by trying to prove to him that she is every bit as intelligent and qualified to make decisions as he is—and she is! Unfortunately, this showdown at the "Not-so-Okay Corral" has brought nothing but stalemate, stagnancy, and estrangement into Cindy and Rick's relationship. The partners spend most of their efforts competing against each other.

Competing Versus Completing

Cindy and Rick desperately need to discover an accurate understanding of biblical roles in regard to headship and submission. Maybe you do, too.

Don't let the word *role* throw you. It merely means "the assumption of responsibility."

An irate woman approached me at a conference where I was one of the speakers. She was waving my book *Don't Bite the Apple 'Til You Check for Worms*, which I wrote as a practical survival guide for people with questions about love, sex, dating, singleness, and preparing for marriage. By the way this woman was waving the bright blue cover in my face, I immediately guessed that her intentions were not to promote sales.

"I read your book," she spat at me bitterly.

"Oh, really? How did you like it?" The moment the words came out of my mouth, I thought, *Wrong question, Abraham!*

"I think it's sexist," she retorted without hesitation.

"Sexist?" I repeated. My books have been called many things—but never *sexist*.

"Yes, sexist. You believe in distinct roles for men and women, and that's sexist and chauvinistic. I believe men and women are equal, and no man will ever tell me what to do."

"Well, I believe men and women are equal, too, but I also believe that God has designed us to fulfill different roles. Those roles aren't meant to be contentious but complementary."

"See? That's what I mean. Roles are sexist."

I realized I was not going to persuade the woman, so I thanked her for her opinion and went on to the next person waiting to speak to me. But I've met that same woman in a host of different places and with many different faces. Somehow, in all the furor over male-female equality, we have been duped into believing that any delineation of roles is sexist and to be avoided. Nothing could be further from the truth.

God intends for the husband-and-wife relationship to be harmonious and complementary. The phrase *my other half* is not a bad way of saying it. To help bring a couple together as creative counterparts, He has established a pattern of the husband as "head" (source), and the wife as "heart" (support) of the family. *Headship* does not mean "boss." It means "servant."

Submission does not mean "subjection." In fact, the Apostle Paul clearly points out that in marriage, submission must be mutual. Before he says a word about wives submitting to their husbands, Paul instructs both men and women to "be subject to one another in the fear of Christ" (Ephesians 5:21).

In mutual submission, two partners refuse to play power games. They do not demand, command, or coerce. They serve each other. They willingly give themselves to one another out of love, trust, and respect.

There is nothing wrong with roles and responsibilities in marriage. Perhaps the real question is, "Who will take responsibility for what?" Roles in marriage have little to do with intelligence, authority, or worth. Basically, I believe, God designed them for better efficiency and function and to provide a unifying order to the home. When roles of headship and submission are divisive for a couple, you can be certain that somebody's understanding is deficient, or somebody's attitude or actions are out of whack.

A husband and wife are supposed to be a team, working together for the common good. A friend of mine is fond of saying, "There is no *I* in *team*." You serve in different *roles* as you work toward shared *goals*. God intends for marriage to involve teamwork.

You can see this even in the physical reproduction process. Obviously, God designed the woman's body, not the man's, to bear children. Nevertheless, despite all the breakthroughs in biochemistry, it still requires a man's involvement to have a baby. Thus, the common perception has been that a wife is to be the childbearer and a husband should be the primary provider. This does not mean that a woman's total value comes from having babies any more than a man's total value is derived from his job, although both statements have a measure of truth. Nor does it imply that a wife cannot pursue a career apart from keeping her home. It does mean that in most cases, if a couple has children, they will probably choose the more traditional pattern of the wife as homemaker and the husband as provider.

Nowadays, many wives who have chosen to maintain a career outside the home are finding that it's a tough balancing act. For many working wives, having it all means *doing* it all.

According to Arlie Hochschild, author of *The Second Shift*, "The household roles of men and women have not evolved along with their work lives: It is women who still bear the greater responsibility for child care, cooking and cleaning." Hochschild told *People* magazine (September 4, 1989), "We're in a stalled revolution. There is the myth of this happy, liberated working woman, briefcase in one hand; child in the other. The notion is that all the necessary changes have occurred, but they haven't."

Hochschild believes that most men have plenty of room

for improvement when it comes to helping with household responsibilities:

> I found that four out of five men don't share the work at home. Most men do something, but they're less likely to do the daily chores, like fixing breakfast or dinner. They are more likely to do chores that can be put off to an odd moment, like changing oil in the car or mowing the lawn. Women are more likely to do two things at once. They will be cooking and talking to their child, or on the phone and paying the bills.

This does not preclude a Christian woman from working outside her home or pursuing a career other than homemaking. The description of a godly woman in Proverbs 31 makes this clear. In fact, she should be appreciated: "Her children rise up and bless her; Her husband also, and he praises her, saying: 'Many daughters have done nobly, But you excel them all' " (Proverbs 31: 28, 29).

Surely it is possible for a woman to have both: a happy home and a satisfying career. Still, when faced with decisions that pit her family against her self-interest, the godly woman will keep her family up front in her priorities. She must ask the tough questions, "How will this affect my family?" and "What will this do to my relationship with my husband and children?"

Some things simply aren't worth the sacrifice required. You can't do it all. A wife's career or contribution to the family finances should never come at the expense of, or to the detriment of, her relationship with her husband and children.

Certainly, no one person can be a wife, mother, student, career woman, entrepreneur, maid, cook, nurse, taxi service, and accountant without help. That's where we guys need to set aside our pride and pick up a dustcloth. Washing dishes or running a vacuum cleaner won't harm your masculinity. Your wife is not your maid or your slave; she is your partner and your equal. As the bumper sticker says, "Men of quality are not threatened by women seeking equality."

Does Anybody Really Enjoy Housework?

Probably not, but here are a few suggestions to help you tolerate the tedious tasks while you create the type of homelife you hoped for when you first married.

1. *Talk with your mate about your housekeeping expectations.* As odd as it may seem, many couples never discuss the mundane, minor tasks that need to be done around the house. They simply get irritated when their spouses fail to guess correctly. Be sure to discuss your attitude toward housekeeping as well as who does what.

It isn't fair to expect your mate to work all day, making a better living for the two of you, and still be a meticulous housekeeper. Face it: if you want to be a two-income couple and have a spotless house as well, you'd better hire a maid.

Ask yourself, "What do I really do around here to help reduce the load of chores? Am I sharing the burden? Am I doing too much and allowing my spouse to be lazy? Are my expectations realistic for us, or am I assuming my spouse will take care of all the things that were taken care of for me as I was growing up at home?"

Are you satisfied with your present arrangement? If not,

what changes would you like to see your mate make? Write those things down. What could *you* do differently to help ease your spouse's load? Write those things down, too, and then, at a calm, convenient opportunity, take out your two lists and talk them over with your partner. Your mate may be surprised at what you consider his or her responsibilities, but you will gain nothing by keeping your lists to yourself.

2. *Evaluate each of your gifts and talents and then divide your domestic responsibilities accordingly.* If one of you is more adept at dealing with mathematics, it only makes sense to put that person in charge of the checkbook. If one of you is more mechanically inclined than the other, that partner may enjoy fixing appliances or working on the car.

In our home, I wouldn't ask Angela to paint the porch. On the other hand, she wouldn't want me to choose our wallpaper. Similarly, I can iron a shirt or press a pair of pants when necessary, but it wouldn't be practical for me to do the entire laundry. It takes me about fifteen to twenty minutes to iron every shirt. Furthermore, I doubt that Angela would trust my hot ironing hand when it comes to her silk dresses.

Few people actually enjoy taking out the garbage or scrubbing floors. Cleaning the commode does not normally rank in the top ten on most people's lists of "Favorite Saturday Morning Diversions." Still, it's a dirty job . . . but somebody has to do it.

Granted, you can't always equitably divide up the household chores, but it does help to remember that you and your partner are a team. Put the best team member in the position where he or she is most comfortable and effective.

Some couples not only split chores; they also split the days on which they perform those chores. "I'll take out the garbage on Monday, Wednesday, and Friday and you take it out on Tuesday, Thursday, and Saturday." Or, "I'll get the garbage; you can wash the dishes." Other couples divide responsibilities according to week or some other agreed-upon frequency. The important thing is to have some sort of understanding as to who is going to do what and when.

3. *Never nag or criticize your partner's housekeeping habits.* As a general rule, you should never criticize your spouse for *anything*; instead, replace criticism with positive, constructive statements. A few words of praise or well-placed compliments may work wonders!

If you berate your partner's efforts at helping with a chore, don't be surprised if you hear, "Hey, if you don't like it, do it yourself!"

Instead of dragging your partner through the mud, why not try making household chores a more relaxed activity that the two of you can do together? Put on some of your favorite music while you both pitch in to make the beds or dust the furniture or wash the windows.

One husband told me, "We have some of our most intimate conversations while we are doing the dishes together. You can be sure that's one place where the kids won't bother us!"

On the other hand, avoid comments such as these: "When are you ever going to do something around here?" or "If I didn't work night and day, nothing would ever get done in this place!" Nagging, criticizing, and chronic complaining will only cause your spouse to have less enthusiasm for household chores.

4. *Be flexible and recognize each other's equality.* Nowhere in the Bible does it say it is a woman's job to do all the cooking or to change all the baby diapers. True servant leaders and true servant lovers want to help when and where they can.

If one plan for dividing household responsibilities doesn't work, try another. Be sensitive and keep an open mind. Make certain you don't allow housework to consume you or to rob you of so much energy that you have little or no time left to enjoy each other. Who really cares if there is never a speck of dust on top of the refrigerator if you lose your partner or your children?

Emphasize your equality in the marriage relationship by choosing to serve each other. Although your roles may differ, as husband and wife you are equal in God's sight. Recognize, relish, and reinforce that fact by honoring, respecting, and serving one another.

7
The Money Pit

Marriage Myth Number Six:
Two people can live as cheaply as one. Or, "Who cares about money? Love is all we need."

"Sure, two can live as cheaply as one . . . as long as one doesn't eat!"

John Abraham

● ● ● ● ● ● ● ● ● ● ● ●

Few things impact a marriage as much as money. Most people do not get married for money, unless they are extremely foolish or they are unscrupulous connivers. Nevertheless, money is the leading cause of arguments among newlyweds and ranks as one of the top three sources of perpetual complaint and intense marital problems between partners who have been married for a number of years. (The other areas are sex and communication.)

In his book *Debt-Free Living* (Moody, 1989), financial adviser Larry Burkett estimates that "approximately 50 percent of all first marriages fail, and finances are listed as the leading cause of divorce by a factor of four to one over any other cause, including infidelity." This problem is particularly devastating to young married couples. Burkett reports, "Nearly 80 percent of divorced couples between the ages of twenty and thirty state that financial problems were the primary cause of their divorce." Money has a way of bringing out the worst in people.

According to Anthony Pietropinto and Jacqueline Simenauer, authors of *Husbands and Wives: A Nationwide Survey of Marriage* (Time Books, 1979), it doesn't make a difference whether a couple has a lot of money or a little. Money matters, and it matters a lot! In fact, the less money people have, the more arguments they have about financial matters.

Money Talks . . . but What Is It Saying?

Maybe one of the reasons money matters so much is that for most people, money means power. The person who controls the purse strings calls the shots. For some people, money means security. For others, it is a means of control. Sometimes it signifies independence. Often it is viewed as a source of status or self-esteem. When you realize how important money is to people, it is no wonder so many marriages are foiled by financial frays.

Perhaps even more fundamental than questions such as "How will we make our money?" and "How should we spend or save it?" is the emotional significance money holds for most people. The real issue is trust:

"Do you really trust me enough to put your money where your mouth is?"

"How much do I trust you?"

"Does what belongs to you really belong to me?"

"Are we in this thing together?"

Two factors make these questions more complicated for modern couples. One, the fresh emphasis upon male-female equality may have dispelled forever the notion that the husband is to be the provider and the wife is to be the protected. Second, many modern-day men and women are marrying much later in life than previous generations did. Consequently, they are bringing to their marriages more financial resources—perhaps a home, a car, a bank account, or investments. Conversely, many are bringing along a house payment, a car payment, an overdrawn checking account, or a poor business investment.

Not surprisingly, we have witnessed the rise of "prenuptial agreements," legal documents that specifically spell out the financial arrangements to which a couple has agreed upon before entering into marriage. Real romantic, huh? Furthermore, disputes over who gets what are often based upon a legitimate fear that the couple's future together will inevitably lead to divorce court.

You may be reluctant to admit it, but your money is you, and you are your money. By this, I mean it is quite simple to see where your priorities and commitments are merely by examining how you spend your money. Gary Chapman suggests that your financial patterns even reveal some insights into how you honor God in your life. Chapman says in *Toward a Growing Marriage*, "One's relationship with God may best be judged by his check stubs, not his church attendance."

In marriage, you should no longer talk about *my* money and *your* money; you must begin to think, speak, and act in terms of *our* money. Likewise, the day you said, "I do," you inherited all of your partner's debts and liabilities, if not legally then at least emotionally. Neither you nor your mate can be in debt without having it affect your marriage relationship.

113

If money matters so much in marriage, why are we so hesitant to talk about it? Many Christians refuse to talk frankly about finances for fear of being considered greedy. It is often subtly implied, "If you were more spiritual-minded, you wouldn't be so concerned about material possessions." But consider this: Jesus talked more about money, and a person's attitude toward and relationship to it, than He did any other subject. He specifically used money to illustrate principles in almost half of His parables. Jesus well understood how intimately linked people can become to their wallets.

Understand, money itself is never the problem. Many people misquote the Apostle Paul as saying, "Money is the root of all evil." The apostle's warning actually was, "For the *love* of money is a root of all sorts of evil, and some by longing for it have wandered away from the faith, and pierced themselves with many a pang" (1 Timothy 6:10, italics added). There is nothing wrong with having money; the problems come when money has *you*.

Marriage does not solve your money problems; it exacerbates them. If you lived for money before you married, you will probably continue to battle your lust for the bucks. If you were a poor money manager before your wedding, your marriage will not magically imbue you with fiscal expertise—unless you married an accountant!

"My wife thinks money grows on trees!" complained Pete, a man married for over ten years. "We have a simple relationship when it comes to money: I make it and she spends it! I knew she spent a lot of money on clothes and cosmetics before we were married, but I figured after our wedding, she'd be able to live on a budget. Boy, was I ever wrong!"

Insufficient Funds and Insufficient Fun

For many couples, the "Great American Dream" has turned into the "Great American Nightmare." Frequently, the cause of this is the common misconception that a newly married couple should be able to acquire in three months all of the material possessions it took their parents thirty years to purchase. Many couples want to start their marriages with new furniture, a new stove, refrigerator, microwave, dishwasher, and other appliances. If their income is insufficient, rather than saving or sacrificing, many couples will resort to credit-card purchases or bank loans.

Angela and I stepped into that pit at the beginning of our marriage. First of all, we wanted a wedding that we would enjoy and remember. Something special. Unique. Distinctively "us." That's when we decided to get married on Mackinac Island, a lovely but expensive resort area in northern Michigan. In a weird way, we felt we were being frugal; our first choice was Hawaii!

Furthermore, like many young couples, we didn't relish the idea of furnishing our little apartment with hand-me-downs and other people's castoffs. It was tough enough to make do in our three tiny rooms, let alone having to decorate in "Early American Garage Sale."

By the time Angela and I paid for our wedding, the renovation and refurnishing of our apartment, and our honeymoon, we were over ten thousand dollars in debt to banks, credit-card companies, and local retailers. To some people, that amount might have been a drop in the bucket. To us, it was like looking up at the bottom of the bucket from the bottom of the ocean. Ten thousand dollars

115

seemed like ten million. We began to learn some hard lessons about being in debt.

Almost immediately, we discovered one of the obvious consequences of debt: insufficient funds. There never seemed to be enough money to pay our bills. We quickly learned the fine art of juggling our creditors, which for us meant throwing all of the bills up in the air and paying only those that landed face-up ("It must be the Lord's leading!"). Before long, our incessant battle with insufficient funds began to take its toll upon our relationship. Even though we were giddily in love with each other, we began to suffer from that common newlywed malady: *insufficient fun*. Money was simply not available to do many of the fun things we wanted to do.

The Dangers of Debt

What did debt do to us? First of all, it shackled us and sapped our spiritual energy. We found that we were in spiritual bondage because of financial bondage. Because strong monetary chains tied us to this world, we felt paralyzed in our personal spiritual progress and stunted in our spiritual growth as a couple. Debt has a tendency to do that to a person. It makes you feel as if you have sold your future down the river—and in a sense, you have.

Beyond that, financial bondage strapped us down and robbed us of our freedom of choice, both practically and spiritually. For example, practically, we were limited as to where we could go and what we could do on vacation—if we could afford to take a vacation! Our debts pretty much dictated our destination, making many of our choices into foregone conclusions.

Spiritually, it became dangerously tempting to disobey the Lord's direction. When you are in debt, you feel less free to follow the Lord's leading, especially if that direction is into an area where you must give up what little security you possess presently. For instance, if the Lord calls you to go to Malaysia as a missionary, you may be tempted to ignore that direction if you are dragging around a ball and chain of financial debt.

Understand: The Bible doesn't say that debt is a sin. But it comes mighty close! Scripture strongly discourages going into debt. Why? Because "The rich rules over the poor, And the borrower becomes the lender's slave" (Proverbs 22:7).

How true that was for Angela and me! Our financial obligations made us feel like slaves—slaves to J. C. Penney; slaves to MasterCard; slaves to Sears; slaves to American Express. As a corollary to our self-inflicted slavery, we soon lost our joy in the Lord. We became frustrated, depressed, worried, introspective, and selfish. In short, we became lousy representatives of, and ambassadors for, Christ. After all, it's tough to talk convincingly about Jehovah-jireh, "the Lord, our provider," when you are buried beneath a mountain of bills.

That was the other thing debt did to us: it made us feel as though we had denied God an opportunity to provide for our needs. We realized that although we talked a pretty good Christian line, we really didn't trust Him as much as we thought. While we prayed beautiful prayers telling Jesus how much we loved Him, we had more faith in First National Bank than we did in the Bank of Heaven; we were more willing to trust in MasterCard than to give the Master charge.

Why would any Christian couple do something so silly? First, because being in debt seems so normal and comes so naturally nowadays. Most of your friends and neighbors are probably in debt up to their ears! Our nation is so far in debt that our government can barely service the interest on its loans. The world economy is built upon debt. So what's the big deal about you or me being in debt?

Furthermore, retailers make it so easy to purchase items on time payments, items you really couldn't afford if you had to pay for them with cash. The advertisements assault our senses: "Buy now, pay later!" (Which is to say, "Buy now and pay forever, at eighteen percent interest!")

The billboard for a local business boasts, "No down payment necessary!" ("We'll just add that to your monthly payment.")

Here's an ad that you often see during the Christmas season: "No payment due until February!" Have you ever bought something on those terms and then been absolutely flabbergasted at how quickly February came rolling around that year?

Holidays are particularly dangerous for couples prone to credit expenditures. The Labor Day flags have hardly been put away before the first blitz of Christmas advertisements begins to flood your mailbox, a virtual deluge of opportunities to plunge yourself deeper into debt. With increased catalog sales in this country and the advent of several television shopping networks, you no longer even have to go to the mall; you can indulge in "shop lusting" right in the comfort of your living room.

Many of the ads play upon our emotions and sentimentalities. Some of my least favorite commercials are the diamond ads that imply if I truly loved my wife, I'd go out and buy her a new diamond for Christmas—a diamond of "a karat or more." Right behind those spots on my list of least favorites is a watch commercial in which a spouse receives a lovely watch as a gift from his or her partner, then with a slightly pained expression, says to the camera in a wistful voice, "I was really hoping for. . . ."

If you are susceptible to such ploys, you might as well start drawing your financial picture with red ink. You are an advertiser's dream! The issue soon slides from "Do we *need* it?" to "Do we *want* it?" Most of us don't get into debt because of our needs; it is usually our desires that cause the trouble.

A second reason many Christian couples succumb to the seductions of financial debt is impatience. We are simply unwilling to wait upon God. Often, we are reluctant to even pray about whether or not He really wants us to have that item in question. So what do we do?

Charge! We charge right out and purchase that indulgence on credit, or we borrow money from a bank.

One woman's comment may sound familiar to you. She rationalized, "Well, I prayed about making that purchase, and God didn't answer. So, I went out and bought it on credit."

Whoa! Maybe God did answer. Maybe He was saying, "No!" Or, perhaps He was saying, "Not now." Possibly, His answer was, "I want to give you something better," or "No, that thing will not be good for you," or "It's not a wise purchase," or "That thing may become an idol in your life." Often, we think prayer is a one-way street. We hurl our hurried requests at God and then go ahead and do what we want. It's not enough to say, "Well, I prayed about it." The main question is, "What did God say?"

Once we know what God has said about a matter, then the issue becomes, "Do we really trust Him?" After all, who needs God to supply supernaturally if we can talk a banker into giving us what we want?

Please understand: Borrowing is not inherently sinful; banks are not bastions of the "evil empire," and bankers are not bad people. But when you trust the bank as your supplier more than you trust God, borrowing money can become an almost blasphemous act.

Before you and your spouse make that next major purchase, it would be wise to ask the Lord for direction in two areas: "Do You want us to have this thing right now?" and "How do You want to provide it for us?" Keep in mind that what He wants in your life and how He plans to provide for it may be radically different from your approach. One of the great lessons Angela and I learned through our financial struggles was how to trust God and to wait upon Him for His perfect timing and His perfect method of providing for our needs; and yes, even for the desires of our hearts (*see* Psalm 37:3–11).

Too Many Gifts Can Bust the Budget

Most couples who are in debt have no idea how much it is actually costing them to live each month. Oh, sure, they may know how much money they *make*, but to pin them down on exactly how much they *spend* is another story. You may think the obvious answer is, "Well, if they are in debt, they must be spending what they make." Think again. Indebted couples spend *far more* than they make. Most Americans owe more than they own!

It is not that indebted couples don't have a financial

plan (although many do not). More frequently, a couple is too idealistic in their plan. They include the house payment and the car payment but conveniently forget about details such as taxes and maintenance on the house and insurance, licenses, and repairs on the automobile. Utilities, personal insurance, medical expenses, recreation, and tithes should all be counted when you begin tallying up your costs of living. Oh, yes; what about food, clothing, and gasoline? Vacations? Business trips? Meals eaten away from home? They all add up.

One budget buster that periodically blew Bill and Linda offtrack was birthdays. Linda has a large family: four brothers, three sisters, and her mom and dad. Buying birthday presents for each person in Linda's family became a sore spot for Bill. It wasn't that he didn't love Linda's relatives, nor was Bill being stingy. But almost every month, another birthday gift left a gaping hole in their budget. Christmas was a catastrophe. When Bill and Linda totaled their gift expenditures for the year, they were shocked to discover they had spent over twelve hundred dollars on presents, and that price tag did not include gifts they had purchased for each other!

At the next family gathering, Bill and Linda hesitantly broached the possibility of drawing names for next Christmas. To their surprise, the rest of the family expressed delight. Then Bill took things a step further. "Look, folks," he said. "It's not that we love you any less, but Linda and I have decided that we can no longer afford to buy everyone an individual birthday present. So this year, we'll send you a card or something, but please understand; we're trying to get our finances in order." Bill paused to take a deep breath, but before he could continue, the other family members broke out in spontaneous applause. Apparently they, too, had felt the financial crunch of giving gifts to each family member.

Maybe you aren't spending twelve hundred dollars on birthday and Christmas gifts, or maybe you are spending more. Regardless, you must incorporate that amount into your budget and plan for those expenses. Be realistic rather than idealistic when you establish your budget. Otherwise, those unaccounted-for expenses will hit when you least expect them, and often, when you can least afford them.

When Should You Have a Baby?

A more common budget buster for most couples is the birth of a baby. You might think this is a strange place to discuss having children, but it's a subject that needs to be dealt with, so let's do it now.

You may or may not have planned for your bundle of joy, but the simple fact is this: Babies cost money. Certainly, financial considerations are not of paramount importance when deciding whether or not, or when, to have children. Nevertheless, don't be naive. If two cannot live as cheaply as one, neither can three . . . or four . . . or five!

How will you know when you are ready for children, and how will that impact upon you economically? Numerous factors should be considered. Most of them converge around three poles: physical factors, emotional factors, and financial factors. Underlying all of these areas, of course, is the spiritual foundation upon which your relationship is being built.

The physical factor is a common concern nowadays, especially for the mother. Unquestionably, women are waiting until later in life to have children. According to the National Center on Health Statistics, quoted in *Today's Marriage* magazine (October 1986), "The number of women between the ages of 30 and 39 who are having their *first* child has more than tripled during the last ten years."

The reasons for this trend may be obvious. First, people are postponing marriage longer than they did in past generations. Second, thanks to modern methods of contraception, many couples are making the matter of having a child more of a choice than a chance. Third, more women are working outside the home and want to wait until they have established some sense of career stability before taking a pregnancy leave. Fourth, many couples are carefully considering the benefits of being older parents, such as a deeper, more mature relationship between them, their readiness to pour themselves into raising a child, and the increased financial security that hopefully accompanies age.

Nevertheless, the biological clock continues to run, and every year past the age of twenty-five, a woman's fertility decreases. This does not mean that she can't have a baby, merely that the chance of her getting pregnant is less. Consequently, it may take an older couple longer than a younger couple to conceive a child.

Doctors are divided on their opinions about older women giving birth, but most concede that there is an increase in danger to the mother commensurate with her age. Furthermore, it is generally agreed that the older the woman, the greater the risk of giving birth to a baby with a birth defect such as Down's syndrome.

For older dads, the physical issue often takes a different

form. Many wonder if they will have the energy and stamina required to raise a child. Said one new father in his early forties, "I have nightmares about needing a cane to walk down the aisle with my daughter on her wedding day!"

Of course, the most important questions regarding the right time to have a baby revolve around your marriage relationship itself. Are you emotionally and spiritually mature enough to accept the mammoth responsibility of bringing another child into this world? Are you totally committed to each other, and is your relationship functioning at a reasonably high quality? Do you really desire a baby or do you regard a child as a means to an end?

Often a man or a woman wants a baby to make up for what is lacking in the marriage relationship. This is almost always disastrous for both the parents and the child. Bluntly, if you are not making it as husband and wife, having a baby will only exacerbate your problems and put more stress on an already shaky foundation. Rarely does becoming parents bring long-term improvement to a muddled marriage. You would be wise to work on being a good husband or wife before you take on the additional responsibilities of becoming a father or a mother.

The third major factor to consider before having a baby brings us full circle, back to the financial area. Can you afford to have a baby? According to the U.S. Department of Agriculture (the same folks who keep track of how much it costs to raise a healthy crop of corn!), it now takes over $150,000 to raise a healthy baby up to voting age. This figure does not include any special medical care required, day care, preschool educational programs, or—are you ready for this?—a day of college education. Obviously, babies cost big bucks!

Now, here's where things get sticky. In today's financial climate, the two-income marriage has become the norm, and often the necessity, rather than a rarity or a luxury. To add another mouth to feed and body to clothe, as well as all the other multitudinous expenses involved in raising a child, while at the same time slashing your total income, is going to require some major financial planning and adjusting.

The reason it is necessary to consider these factors within a financial framework should be obvious, yet surprisingly, many couples seem to be blind to it. At some point, and for some season, if you have children, you are going to be a one-income family. If your budget is built around both husband and wife working, you had better make some immediate life-style adjustments before having children, or else prepare for the big crash. Every baby is a blessing from God, but if you are financially burdened before your child's birth, your newborn may not be the only member of your family crying himself or herself to sleep.

How to Blast Your Budget . . .
Buy a New Car

Compared with having a baby, buying a new car is a piece of cake! Ask any mother. Better still, ask any dad. Nevertheless, one of the quickest and easiest means of bombing your budget into oblivion is by borrowing money to purchase a new automobile.

"New-car-itis," a disease that normally affects young men in their teens, is temporarily cured by the purchase of an old clunker but then periodically reappears as a man ages, often with the price for treatment becoming increasingly expensive with time. Rare is the woman who truly understands this male malady.

Most men have been indoctrinated since they were young boys that "you are what you drive." Therefore, for many fellows, a car is not transportation; it is status. When a guy spends all day waxing an automobile, he is not only weatherproofing the paint; he is polishing his self-image. He sees himself in that car in more ways than one!

For you women who can't comprehend such a childish concept, try to understand that a man feels about his automobile much the way you feel about your home. He could care less if one of the kids spills ink on your living room carpet (unless he has to pay to have it cleaned or replaced), but just let one of those little tykes with sticky fingers touch the leather upholstery on his dashboard, and then watch the sparks fly!

Even after he has been married for a number of years, a man does not dream of driving down the street in a station wagon loaded down with a pack of screaming kids. He pictures himself and "his woman" gently easing through traffic in a red sports coupe, waving to the admiring passersby as if the two of them were grand marshals of the Rose Bowl Parade.

Unfortunately, the harsh truth is this: With today's automobiles selling for the price of a home in the 1960s, the average young couple cannot afford the luxury of buying a brand-new car, especially when you consider the peripheral expenses that go into the purchase, such as license, inspection, maintenance, gasoline, insurance, and oh, yes, the monthly payment. Sorry, guys, but your best bet would be to purchase a good two- or three-year-old used car directly from an owner you know personally.

Ron Blue, a Christian financial consultant and a certified public accountant, did a study to determine the most economical car he could ever drive. His results shocked even him. He reports in *Master Your Money* (Nelson, 1986):

> After studying this whole issue of buying automobiles, I came to two conclusions: the cheapest car anyone can ever own is always the car *they presently own*, unless it is sold and the proceeds reinvested in a lower priced car; and the longer a car is driven, the cheaper it becomes to operate.

Inevitably, that not-so-new car of yours will tend to act up or break down at just the wrong moment. Nevertheless, you must not yield to the temptation to chuck the clunker over the closest cliff.

Keep in mind the Scripture that says, "Tribulation brings about perseverance; and perseverance, proven character; and proven character, hope" (Romans 5:3, 4). Also keep in mind that even if you spend one hundred dollars per month on repairs to the clunker, it is still a lot less expensive than two hundred dollars to five hundred dollars per month in car payments. Granted, it's tough to put a price tag on your frustration when a car fails, but if you ever hope to be debt-free, my advice is pay your car off and drive it until it dies. Put the money you would have used for a car payment into the bank each month, and before you know it, you will have saved enough money to buy another good used car—without plunging into debt.

The Big One . . . Buying a House

In 1970, the median price of a new house in the United States was $23,386; by 1979 the average price of a new house shot up to $64,700; at the beginning of the 1990s, that same house sells for over $130,000! Unfortunately, the average income has not kept pace with housing costs; the average American income today barely nudges past the $24,000 mark.

Even with a thirty-year mortgage, many couples are spending over 70 percent of their income on housing costs. At the same time, most financial institutions estimate that annual housing expenses, including taxes, mortgage payment, insurance, maintenance, and utilities should not exceed 25 to 30 percent of a couple's annual income. Obviously, if you are an average couple with an average income, and you desire to purchase an average home in this country, you have a much-greater-than-average problem!

What can you do? First, decide what it is you really need in your housing. Do you *really* need five bedrooms, four baths, and a study, or could you get by with less? Write down what you and your spouse feel are minimum requirements concerning amount of space, neighborhoods, schools, access to your job, and anything else that affects your decision. It is important to spell these items out in as specific detail as possible. If you don't know what you both are looking for, you are liable to be easily influenced by an overzealous real estate agent.

Second, weigh the advantages and disadvantages to renting rather than purchasing. Generally, if you know you will be moving in less than five years, renting a place makes more sense than buying. Don't be deceived by those dubious advisers who vociferously encourage you to take advantage of all the tax breaks the government grants to homeowners.

Granted, renting an apartment or a previously owned house is not as glamorous as buying or building a place, but there are definite advantages. For example, by renting, you know fairly well what your monthly expenses will be, since maintenance and repair costs normally land on the landlord's desk. If you rent in an apartment complex, you may have amenities you could not afford to purchase, such as a swimming pool, fitness center, or community clubhouse. Furthermore, you have no concerns about selling your property if you decide to move.

On the other hand, you may feel as though you are dumping money down the drain by renting. If you were purchasing a home, hopefully you would be building some equity, or resale value, as you make the monthly payments. These and other considerations need to be thoroughly thought through before making your decision.

Once you have decided that it is to your financial advantage to purchase a house, the real fun begins. You now get to play that popular game enjoyed by millions of couples every weekend: "Let's Find a Place in Our Price Range!" This assumes, of course, that you have already made it through the preliminary round: "What *Is* Our Price Range?" Nobody pays much attention to the preliminaries, nowadays. Maybe that's why many couples are "house poor."

If you actually survive the painful process of roaming around untold acres of property, arm in arm with a real estate agent, you may be ready to do battle with your banker.

Besides the huge amount of interest banks charge you for borrowing their money (which you can semiunderstand since, after all, it is their money, or at least their depositors' money), they have devised dozens of "incidental" fees that you almost need a second mortgage to pay. First, they sock you with a "loan origination fee," which is what you pay for the privilege of walking through their doors and doing business with them. Then come the appraisal fee, credit report fee, inspection fee, recording fee, title fee, abstract fee (aren't they all?), fee-fee, fee for your banker's foreign vacation, and fees for almost anything else they can dream up. Most lenders even charge you a few bucks for the paper that tells you how much you're going to have to pay! They call it by a big name—an amortization schedule—which is to hide the fact that you just paid for a ream of paper.

Perhaps the most perplexing of the various "services" provided by your banker for which you have the privilege of paying through your nose is the phenomenon known as "paying points." Although I have queried numerous intelligent, astute financiers, nobody has provided me with a plausible explanation as to why you must pay points when you purchase a home. They all stammer and stumble, mumble and grumble something about the high cost of living, or the new Mercedes they just bought, but no banker has ever adequately answered my questions— at least not to my satisfaction!

I would rather bankers fed me some ridiculous line such as "We need the money to help support anticommunist freedom fighters on the face of the moon" or "We are taking your cash to pay for the training of penguins in Antarctica; we're teaching them to fly."

Lest you get the correct impression that I am somewhat jaded concerning the entire mortgage system, let me qualify my statements by saying I am merely attempting to warn you that buying a home is a big-time budget buster, and the procedure should not be entered into without much prayer and careful consideration. Some people get rich through real estate; many destroy their marriages because of biting off a chunk too big to chew.

Still, I have faith in a small-scale version of the "American Dream" (whatever that is these days). In fact, at this very moment, my wife and I are considering the purchase of a new house . . . provided we can get a mortgage. . . .

How to Get a Grip on Money Before It Strangles You

Let's face it. Getting into debt is simple. It's as easy as riding the down escalator at the mall. Getting out of debt is like trying to walk back up the escalator that is coming down. It can be done, but it takes some real effort.

Here are some suggestions that will help you get out of debt and stay out of debt.

1. *Pray.* Pray first for forgiveness of selfishness, foolishness, and lust (lust not only applies to sex; a lust for *things* can be just as damning as sexual lust).

Debt is rarely caused by a mere lack of money. Debt is, however, a good indicator that something may be wrong at the center of your life that has caused you to slide down the slippery slope of fiscal irresponsibility. Perhaps it was pride that led to your misusing the financial resources God gave you; possibly selfishness played a part. Other culprits could be greed, self-centeredness, self-indulgence,

131

impatience, fear, or lack of personal discipline. Maybe your debts were brought about through immaturity, foolishness, or lack of faith. Regardless, your first few steps toward financial freedom will be realizing that your debts indicate spiritual needs as well as monetary: taking responsibility for your mistakes, repenting of those sins, and asking God for His forgiveness. As with any forgiveness, if it is to be effective, you must forgive any other people who might be involved and forgive yourself as well. You will do yourself no favor by verbally beating yourself again and again, saying, "How could I have been so foolish?" Let it go, and trust God for a new start. Pray also for wisdom to make the right choices in the future and the courage to take the next step of obedience, as God directs you. Ask God to help you make the necessary changes that will cure the problems rather than merely assuage the symptoms.

2. *You must spend less than you earn!* It sounds silly, yet most married couples in debt ignore this basic principle. If you ever hope to get free from financial bondage, you must stop overspending! It's simple: You must have more money coming in each month than you are shelling out. Otherwise the downward spiral will continue.

Many couples find they have too much *month* left at the end of their *money*. This pattern must be reversed, but that's the tough part. The only way you can spend less is by changing something in your life-style. Admit it: you didn't get into debt by making wise choices or doing everything correctly. If you continue your same patterns of spending, you can expect the same patterns of debt.

Break that bondage by beginning immediately to keep track of every penny that comes in and every cent that

goes out. Many good books on budgeting are available at
your local bookstore. Your pastor may be able to help, or
perhaps there are some individuals in your church who
are competent to counsel you and are willing to share their
financial expertise with you. Do not, however, seek unbiblical counsel.

3. *Sell what you can, and use any income earned to pay your
bills.* Maybe you are driving a car that is fancier than what
you really need or can afford. Sell it and get a good used
car; then put the profits toward paying your bills. Don't
use the money you made from selling the car to go on
vacation or to buy a new stereo system. *Make payments on
the bills!*

Look around your garage, your basement, or your spare
closet. Many items of interest and value may be hiding
there, just waiting for you to set a date, put up a sign, and
have a garage sale. Lay down your pride and do it! Who
cares if the neighbors sniff, "Well! Times must be tough
next door; they're even selling Aunt Martha's favorite af-
ghan." Times *are* tough next door, and they will get
tougher if you don't take action.

Furthermore, the stigma formerly attached to garage
sales and yard sales is now almost nonexistent. A wealthy
friend told me he has no qualms about driving his Mercedes to a garage sale. "People want to sell some of the
nicest things," he said.

4. *If necessary, set up a repayment schedule with your creditors.* Granted, this pinches your pride. But if you are serious about escaping the financial quagmire, it may be the
best way of pulling yourself out of debt.

Go directly to your creditors, if they have local offices,
and explain your situation (write to those you cannot visit

personally). It is important to take a written debt-repayment plan with you to show what you can honestly afford to pay. Sincere promises are wasted words when talking to a creditor. Most likely, he or she has heard every sob story in the book; you need a *plan*. This plan should present proof of your income and a general statement of your bills. Emphasize to your creditor that you *will* pay this bill, and provide a fair estimate of what you think you can pay every month. As a Christian, you do not have any other option. The Bible exhorts, "The wicked borrows and does not pay back, But the righteous is gracious and gives" (Psalm 37:21). If you incur a debt, you are obligated to pay, unless your lender or creditor willingly releases you from that burden.

In most cases, I believe bankruptcy is a second-best solution for a Christian couple. Even though the government says it is okay, and society no longer looks askance at a couple who declares bankruptcy, the residual effects are almost always negative: the loss of personal respect, the loss of integrity, and a gnawing sense of guilt that you have cheated your creditors out of what you owed them.

Larry Burkett, author of *Debt-Free Living*, concurs:

> In some situations a voluntary bankruptcy is acceptable, but only in the context of trying to protect the creditors—never in the context of trying to avoid repayment. A Christian needs to accept the hard truth that God allows him no alternative to keeping his vows. That is why the Bible warns him often to be careful before making vows. "It is better that you should not vow than you should vow and not pay" (Ecclesiastes 5:5).

If you will take the courageous step of approaching your creditors, you may be surprised to discover they are willing to help. Your creditors want to be paid, pure and simple. Most would prefer *not* to have to turn your account over to a collection agency because the creditors will lose money—often up to half the amount owed.

If you can present a plan whereby the creditor can be assured that payment is forthcoming, even if the amount is less than originally expected, or the time span is longer, most (not all) lenders will be as lenient as possible. Hint: It helps to take a third party (a legitimate financial counselor) with you when you visit your creditor. The lender will be more likely to take your repayment plan seriously if he or she knows that you are accountable to an outside, objective financial counselor.

5. *Pay a little bit on each debt every month.* You may not be able to make large payments, but your creditors will appreciate your attempts to make *consistent* payments. As you progress, concentrate on eliminating the *smallest* debts you owe *first*. Begin knocking them off one by one (your debts, not your creditors!). As you get the smallest bill paid, step up to the next one, and start chipping away at it. Your successes will spur you on until each debt is paid. One caution: Do *not* go out and purchase something else on credit as a reward for paying off a tiny debt. You must discipline yourself. Save your celebrations until you can afford to pay for them—with cash.

6. *Commit "surprise" income ahead of time.* Promise yourself and each other that any unexpected financial blessings are precommitted to your debt-repayment plan. God will honor your efforts to repay your creditors and to live free of financial bondage. As such, couples who take this task

seriously often find that they are the recipients of windfall income. They are getting into God's program, and He is getting involved in theirs.

While I can't guarantee that God is going to dump a truckload of money on your front lawn, I have seen this process work often enough that I am no longer shocked when He provides in some unexpected manner for a couple who are attempting to honor Him in the area of their finances. I still marvel at His generosity, but I am not surprised when Jehovah-jireh lives up to His Name.

Unfortunately, many couples squander His blessings by blowing the unexpected income on some indulgence. Don't do it! Agree ahead of time that if God blesses you with money you didn't expect, He is attempting to help you get out of debt (unless you receive extremely clear direction from the Lord that the money is to be used for some other purpose). This can be an exciting time for you and your spouse, as you begin to see God's hand at work in your finances. But don't expect the Lord to send money in through the front door if you are going to shovel it out the back door! Honor Him and He will honor you.

7. *Keep tithing*. Speaking of honoring God . . . make sure you give the first 10 percent of your income back to the Lord. Certainly, the New Testament indicates that as Lord of your life, He is the rightful Owner of all you have. The 10 percent is merely a token acknowledgment of the fact that you can be trusted as a steward over the other 90 percent. If you are not tithing—giving Him the first 10 percent of your income—start today. Perhaps your failure to tithe is the reason you are in a financial bind.

You may be thinking, *Tithe? How am I supposed to give*

away 10 percent of my income? I can barely pay the telephone bill!

Then disconnect the phone, but don't rob God! Scripture is extremely clear on this matter. The Lord Himself asks the tough question:

> "Will a man rob God? Yet you are robbing Me! But you say, 'How have we robbed Thee?' In tithes and contributions. You are cursed with a curse, for you are robbing Me, the whole nation of you! Bring the whole tithe into the storehouse, so that there may be food in My house, and test Me now in this," says the Lord of hosts, "if I will not open for you the windows of heaven, and pour out for you a blessing until there is no more need. Then I will rebuke the devourer for you, so that it may not destroy the fruits of the ground; nor will your vine in the field cast its grapes," says the Lord of hosts.
>
> Malachi 3:8–11

Notice: Not only does a couple rob God if they refuse to give Him the first 10 percent of their resources; they also rob themselves. The Lord wants to bless them. Beyond that, He invites them to prove Him, to test Him, to check Him out to see if His promise of blessing is true. Furthermore, He promises to "rebuke the devourer" for those who will put Him first in their finances.

Maybe you can identify with Tom Bodett, author of *Small Comforts* (Addison-Wesley, 1987), when it comes to that "devoured" feeling. Bodett observed, "After marrying each other, my wife and I discovered the principle of buy now, pay later. We sold our souls to a 30-year mortgage and a succession of car payments with matching insurance policies. All our disposable income is calculated a year in advance and spent the year before."

Many Christians feel that way. Once you have gotten into debt, the bondage is not going to disappear (unless you go bankrupt, which usually creates another sort of bondage). Yet, guess where a lot of Christians try to save a few dollars? That's right. They rob God to pay Master-Card or some other bill. Consequently, the downhill slide turns into a rapidly accelerating, descending spiral, spiritually, physically, emotionally, and economically. One fellow who came to me seeking counsel described his condition this way:

> Have you ever seen one of those yellow charity cones outside a restaurant? You toss in the penny and it keeps going in smaller circles until it finally slips down the tube. I am that penny.

Sometimes extenuating circumstances may tempt you not to tithe. That's what happened to Ralph.

A few years ago, Ralph suffered a heart attack while on the job, and a second minor attack in the hospital. He was unable to work for over a year, during which time his company benefits ran out, the bills began stacking up, and the family's financial picture continued to grow bleaker by the day. With two kids in college, Ralph could barely make the house payment, even though his wife, Nancy, had gone back to work.

Ralph and Nancy were in a quandary. What should they do? They were being badgered almost daily by bill collectors, yet they believed the first part of their resources, little as they were, belonged to God. Should they stop tithing, take that money, and pay their bills? Or should they continue to tithe and let the creditors wait?

"It just didn't seem honoring to God," Ralph said sincerely, "to give money to our church, which really wasn't facing any major financial crisis, while we were being a horrible testimony to businesses and creditors who had trusted us in good faith." Ralph and Nancy prayed about the matter and decided it would be more honoring to God if they paid their bills than if they paid their tithes.

"That was a mistake," Ralph later admitted. "It might not have been a sin—our hearts were right, our motives were pure—but it sure was a mistake. We were excluding God from an area of our lives where we needed His help the most at the moment: our finances."

Ralph and Nancy decided to tighten their belts even further and began setting aside the first 10 percent of their meager income for God's work. Almost immediately, the Lord began to honor their efforts. Their income began to increase. God gave Ralph back his health by healing his heart. He was able to go back to work at a less pressure-packed job, making a higher wage than he had been receiving previously. In every way, God began to prosper Ralph and Nancy as they put Him first in their finances.

Their story may not be the absolute pattern for you. The question of whether or not to tithe while you are climbing out of debt is one that should be prayerfully and personally answered. Keep in mind, though, that God will not ultimately be in debt to any man or woman. You can't lose by keeping Him in first place in your life—which brings us to the final suggestion for getting out of debt and staying out.

8. *Put God in charge.* Instead of trusting MasterCard, try trusting the Master—not merely in monetary matters, but

in every area of your marriage. Furthermore, acknowledge Jesus as Lord of your individual lives. I encourage married couples to pray together and speak the words aloud, "Jesus, I commit every area of my life to You: our marriage, our checkbook, our plans, our future; by an act of my will, I commit it all to You. Please help us to make wise choices and to live in a way that honors Your Name."

Do these eight principles really work? you may be wondering. Angela and I can bear personal testimony that they do! When we realized our foolish financial mistakes early in our marriage and began to understand the enormous bondage we had brought upon ourselves and the strain money pressures had placed upon our relationship, we decided the only way we could be happy and free was to get out of debt.

It was not an easy job. It took time, discipline, and cooperation, but we were determined. We began incorporating the principles I have shared with you in these pages. At the same time, we instituted two further safeguards: we meticulously avoided using credit cards for purchases, and we paid for *everything* by check. If the money was not in the account, we didn't buy anything.

We sold Angela's brand-new automobile and used the profits to make payments on our bills. We paid a little bit on each debt every month, eliminating the smallest first. The money we saved on stamps to mail the monthly payments seemed like a financial boon to us! It didn't happen overnight, but as we followed our plan, financial freedom began to appear as a real possibility. Inch by grueling inch, we dug out of debt, and then we began the liberating climb out of the money pit. You can, too!

8
Moonlighting

Marriage Myth Number Seven:
Working wives are happy wives! Or, "Honest, honey. I don't mind working two jobs. . . .

"Most of us are motivated each morning to go to work for three main reasons: Visa, MasterCard, and American Express."

Ron Rich

● ● ● ● ● ● ● ● ● ● ● ● ● ●

According to *Time* magazine (December 4, 1989), "Sixty-eight percent of women with children under 18 are in the work force." If you think most of these women are single parents, think again. Psychologists Melvin Kinder and Connell Cowan estimate, in *Husbands and Wives*, that "in nearly 50 percent of all marriages, the wife works." No longer is a career woman viewed as selfish or unconcerned about her family. On the contrary, nowadays, a wife and mom working at a career outside the home is considered normal and necessary. In a weird case of role reversal, women who *don't* work outside their homes are sometimes suspected of being lazy, unmotivated, or unwilling to contribute wholeheartedly to the welfare of the family.

"I didn't really want to go to work and we honestly didn't need the extra money that much," explained Kim, a perky mother in her late twenties, "but all of my friends from school had good jobs, and whenever I was around them, I'd feel as though they regarded me as a second-class woman because I had chosen to remain at home. Finally, I went out and got a job . . . and I hate it!"

Beyond that, an interesting development has taken place among many men regarding their attitude toward working moms and wives. While at first reticent to accept women in the work force, many guys nowadays *expect* their wives to work outside the home, regardless of how many children they have or what ages the children are. What was once a woman's option has now become another source of exasperation, pressure, and exhaustion. Add to this the fact we noted in a previous chapter, that women are still bearing the brunt of housekeeping burdens, and you have a perfect prescription for a physical burnout, a marital blowout, or both.

Furthermore, few working wives receive the appreciation and approval from their husbands they had anticipated prior to entering the work place.

"Sure, he likes the extra money," lamented Louise, "but he doesn't have a clue as to how hard I work for it, and he doesn't give me a whole lot of credit for my accomplishments, either. It's almost as though he takes my working for granted. Whenever I complain about something in the office, he just smirks and says, 'See, I told you it was no picnic out there. Now you know what I mean.' "

The time has come to ask, Is this system working? Are working wives *really* happy wives?

Granted, the issue of whether or not women can compete in the marketplace has been answered with a resounding yes. Women have proven themselves every bit as competent and capable as their male counterparts in the work place. In some fields, they have demonstrated that they might be even better qualified, for example, in professional careers requiring precise tactile abilities.

The question that nags us now is not, *Can* a woman be successful as a wife, mother, and career person? but rather, Is it really worth it? Economically, physically, and spiritually, what price does a wife's outside work extract from her, her marriage, and her relationships with her family—and is that price too high?

Kathy is a thirty-five-year-old successful office manager employed by a thriving company. She has been married for fourteen years to her husband, Bob, whom she knows is cheating on her. They have no children.

For Kathy, the price of her career success has been more than she anticipated:

> I never dreamed we'd turn out this way. When I went to work, I needed the job because we needed the money. After a while, I realized I was no longer working for the money; I was working to feel good about myself. I was successful at work. People liked me. They told me how good I was at what I did. Bob never did that at home. He was always too preoccupied with his own career. He poured himself into his profession, and I poured myself into mine. I guess we've just drifted apart. We don't believe in divorce, but I know he's running around on me and I've not exactly been faithful to him.
>
> When I get home at night, by the time I get dinner ready and do things that need done around the

143

house, I'm too tired for anything else. A lot of nights, I collapse into bed right after dinner. Bob pressures me for sex, but I'm not interested . . . well, I am interested, but I'm just too tired!

We now have an unusual relationship. I get the strokes I need by being admired, affirmed, and appreciated at work, and he gets the sex he needs someplace else. I know it's weird and I'm scared to death that he's going to catch some horrible, sexually transmissible disease, but that's the way we live.

Strange, isn't it? I found success and fulfillment at work, but what I really wanted in life was a happy marriage and a few kids to raise. I'd trade my title, the desk, and my name on the office door any day for a husband I could love, honor, and trust.

Certainly, Kathy and Bob might have drifted apart whether or not she had an outside job. Possibly the marriage could be saved if the couple would concentrate on meeting each other's needs at home. Regardless, in Kathy's mind, her marriage to Bob broke down because of her career.

Pinstripes or Pampers?

Many modern women are putting off becoming mothers in order to pursue a career outside the home. Some are foregoing the experience of parenthood altogether, although, according to a survey conducted by the U.S. Census Bureau, nine out of ten American women still hope to have a baby someday. While childlessness may appear as a viable alternative for their non-Christian counterparts, many Christian women get guilt pangs when they remain married without children.

"There are all those stories about barren women in the Bible," Shelly replied when a friend asked her why she decided to have children. "It seemed to me that a husband and wife who didn't have kids were almost cursed."

"Yeah," chimed in her husband, Brent. "And what do you do with those verses that talk about children as a blessing of God? I sure don't want to miss out on His blessing!"

Shelly and Brent broach an interesting subject. Some of the most beloved accounts in the Bible revolve around a husband and wife who could not have children, but then as a sign of the blessing of God, conceived, sometimes miraculously. Abraham and Sarah (Genesis 16:1), Hannah and Elkanah (1 Samuel 1:2), and Zacharias and Elizabeth, parents of John the Baptist (Luke 1:5–7), are examples.

Solomon, said to be the wisest man who ever lived, and a fellow well familiar with male-female relationships, unreservedly declared:

> Behold, children are a gift of the Lord;
> The fruit of the womb is a reward.
> Like arrows in the hand of a warrior,
> So are the children of one's youth.
> How blessed is the man whose quiver is full of them;
> They shall not be ashamed,
> When they speak with their enemies in the gate.
> Psalm 127:3–5

Do you see the vivid picture Solomon is painting with his poetic analogy? Notice, he likens kids to the arrows in a warrior's hand; the quiver to which he refers is the warrior's arrow case. Solomon implies that the really blessed warrior has some kids in his hand and a quiverful, too! When I discovered that the average quiver could accommodate five or more arrows, I began to *quiver* myself!

Still, it is a fact that the Bible links a couple's bearing of children with the blessing of God. This is not to say that every married couple must have children in order to receive His blessing, but it does raise the specter of selfishness for those couples who could conceive but purposely choose a career over kids.

Frequently, the quest for success in one's career becomes surprisingly unsatisfying for many couples who decided against children for professional or economic reasons. Kate Menchley and her husband, Pete, both in their mid-forties, made that sacrifice but are now having second thoughts. While sitting behind her desk in her corner office of a downtown Honolulu skyscraper, Kate described her feelings:

> We both scratched and clawed our way up the corporate ladder, and everybody who knows us considers us fabulously successful. In a sense we are, if all you count is money. But for the past twenty years, Pete and I have been merely existing together in the same house. We both worked hard at our jobs, but we lost touch with each other.
>
> Now, here we are, approaching fifty years of age, and we have finally rediscovered one another. But we still come home to an empty house, filled with nothing but expensive trinkets. No sounds of laugh-

ing children, no squawking babies, no hopes for
grandchildren.

We've considered adoption, but at our age, most
agencies are reluctant to place a baby with us. We
have parties for our employees at our home, and we
always encourage them to bring their children. For a
few wonderful hours, the rooms ring with laughter,
shouting, singing, and, oh yes, sometimes crying and
spilled messes on the carpets. But then, everyone
goes back to their homes and we are left in a dreary
silence.

Sure, Pete and I are successful, but we can't deny that
we missed something by not having children in order
to further our careers.

Kate and Pete's plight is not uncommon. If you think
about it for a moment, you can probably name several
couples close to you who bought the myth of the American dream only to find themselves bankrupt emotionally.
On the other hand, when shocked co-workers asked
Susan, a bright operations manager for a major Christian
ministry, why she would be willing to give up such a
prestigious position in order to have children, she countered, "Because a gold watch can't hug me when I'm old."
Clearly, for many working wives, the paycheck has not
paid off, in terms of fulfillment, nearly as much as motherhood. Those who have attempted the Herculean task of
juggling career craziness with wifely wonders and moth-
ering madness have often found the energy and effort they
expended to be more than they could afford. Carol, a married pediatrician with three children of her own, commented about her combination of duties: "It's a constant

feeling of physical and emotional exhaustion. I feel drained all the time. Sometimes I wish I could just stay home with the kids and be a full-time wife and mother."

But I Can't Afford Not to Work!

I've heard that line from so many working wives I've almost come to believe it as an economic fact of life in the nineties. Nowadays, it takes two people working at jobs outside the home to make financial ends meet. Or does it? Perhaps the answer is not more money coming in but less money flowing out, and in a more disciplined manner.

Certainly, some wives simply enjoy working. They are educated, skilled, qualified, and fulfilled in their jobs, and there is no reason they should not work outside the home if they so desire. However, when a wife feels she is forced to work in order for the family to survive, it is usually a signal that this economic house is not in order.

Often, when a couple gets into a financial bind, the first response is for the wife to find work outside the home. If there are no children, and if the wife is able to obtain a high-paying, professional-type job, this may make sense. If, however, there are children at home who need attention and care, and if the wife is employed at minimum wage or slightly above, it may not be worth it for the wife to work. By the time she pays the taxes on her income, tithes, extra transportation costs (which sometimes include a second car), meals eaten away from home, extra clothes or personal items that she may need simply because she is working outside the home, and baby-sitting or day-care expenses, she may be shocked to discover that her total contribution to the family income is less than 30 percent of what she supposedly "made." On a ten-thousand-dollar-per-year job, she might add only three thousand dollars to the family coffers.

The obvious question that every working mother must ask herself is: "Do I really want to spend forty to fifty hours a week away from my children for only that kind of recompense?" Certainly, most parents would agree that no amount of money is worth losing out with your children. Then why allow them to become day-care orphans or latchkey kids (children who return home from school to an empty house until Mom or Dad gets home from work) for only a few thousand dollars?

Normally, except in extreme hardship cases, the wife should not have to work. In this country, you can survive on one salary; you may not be able to purchase a lot of luxuries, but you can live a decent life. When a wife must work, the family is usually living above their means.

Worshiping the Golden Calf

Some couples create needs that compel a wife to work. Sure, you need a place to live, but do you need that particular house or apartment? Most people nowadays need an automobile. But do you need a new, late-model sports car, or could you get by with a good used car? Yes, of course you need food and clothes, but must you buy name-brand items at the most expensive stores in town?

Our modern thirst for materialism has made a mess of many marriages. The popular slogan "The one who dies with the most toys wins" belies the truth that the marriage with the most toys often dies. Greed kills.

Keith and Cindy's marriage was dying right before their

eyes, but they were too blinded by materialism to see it. They both felt that Cindy had to work in order to support their life-style. Yet even with Cindy working at a full-time, executive-level job, the couple continued to wallow in debt.

Keith and Cindy drove expensive, late-model, foreign automobiles. They lived in an exclusive part of town in a house that far surpassed their needs. Cindy's favorite indoor sport was mall-hopping, and she frequently would spend an entire paycheck on new clothes to wear to work. Similarly, Keith could hardly pass by a stereo store without bringing home the latest tapes, compact discs, and the newest electronic gizmo. He even bought a robot to serve after-dinner drinks.

Keith and Cindy had plenty of nice things, but unfortunately, more things did not bring happiness to their marriage. They were both miserable.

Then one night, as Keith was connecting another piece of electrical wizardry to their television set, he came upon a TV preacher who was talking about how to bring a dead marriage back to life. The Spirit of God grabbed hold of Keith's heart, and he sat down and watched the entire program. When the preacher encouraged his listeners to commit their lives and their marriages to Jesus Christ, Keith prayed along with him.

Later he described his experience: "It was like an explosion of love in my heart. Suddenly, I loved Cindy. I loved everybody! I felt as though a million pounds had been lifted off my shoulders, and for the first time in a long while, I felt free."

Keith shared his new faith with Cindy, and although

skeptical, she agreed to pray with him. Together, they dedicated themselves and their marriage to Christ.

Neither of them was prepared for what happened next. One afternoon, Keith called Cindy at work and suggested they meet at a quiet restaurant for dinner; he said he had an important idea he wanted to talk over with her. Cindy readily agreed and even arranged to leave work early.

At dinner that night, Keith dropped what he thought would be a bomb. "Cindy, I've been thinking a lot this week," he began slowly. "You know we really have more material things than many couples acquire in a lifetime. But the most important thing we have, besides the Lord, is each other. I guess what I'm trying to say is that I don't need all the things, but I do need you."

Tears were welling up in Cindy's eyes as she started to speak, but Keith wasn't done. He continued slowly but with genuine excitement in his voice. "Cindy, what would you think about selling our big house, and with the money we make, buy a nice, cozy, smaller place? We could sell the cars and get one good car and a little puddle-jumper. And, if we both worked hard at disciplining our spending, I think we could make it on just my salary. That way, if you want to stay home, or if you want to work just a few days a week, you can. And Cindy," Keith reached across the table and took Cindy's hand, "maybe we could even have a baby!"

By this time, tears were streaming down Cindy's face. "Yes, yes!" she answered through her tears, as she patted her eyes with a napkin. "It's what I've always wanted, Keith. I thought that if I kept working harder, maybe someday it would happen, but there was always something else we wanted to buy, so I've kept on working. But your idea sounds like the right solution. Let's pray about it and then do what God wants us to do."

Keith and Cindy's strategy may or may not be right for you. You don't need someone else's plan; you want God's plan for *your* marriage. Ask Him what is the most appropriate method of meeting your financial needs. At the same time, you would be wise to ask yourselves, "Are we working to live or living to work?" What are your reasons for having a working wife and mom in the family? Do you really need the money, or are you addicted to material things that require both of you to work full-time to support your habits?

Isn't There a Better Way?

More than ever before, women of the twenty-first century are clamoring for freedom of choice. Ironically, in all the fuss about women's rights, the choice most often overlooked is that of whether or not a wife may employ her privilege of being a mother and a homemaker. Many successful career women would prefer to remain at home and raise their children if—and it is a mighty big *if*—they could maintain the same standard of living on only the husband's salary. Unfortunately, unless you have saved, stolen, or inherited a huge sum of money, that is a most unlikely possibility.

Consequently, many moms are choosing to sequence their life objectives rather than attempt the arduous task of juggling a career and family responsibilities simultaneously. One wise working woman put it this way: "I realized that if God allows me to live a normal seventy-year life span, that is more than enough time to raise a family *and* develop a career. I don't need the pressure of trying to do them both at the same time, so I am leaving my job. I'm going to pour myself into my husband and our kids. Then, when the kids are grown, I will go back to my career. It won't be easy; we've grown accustomed to two paychecks. But we think it will be worth it."

Sequencing your life steps demands that you make tough choices. Some women choose to leave their careers completely; others simply cut back on their work schedules. Other couples reverse the process by pouring themselves into their jobs for the early part of their marriage; then when they have established some measure of financial stability, they can shift gears and focus more attention on family life. Either strategy demands sacrifice, cooperation, and understanding from you and your spouse. One thing is certain: the idea that the contemporary woman can "have it all" without a significant trade-off in quality of life-style and relationships is a myth.

Rather than interrupting their careers during the years of motherhood, more and more women are opting for part-time employment. Especially popular are those job opportunities that allow a woman to work at home—careers such as writing, accounting, business consulting, phone sales, and many more. Mail-order businesses are thriving. Home craft businesses keep many wives and mothers actively involved as entrepreneurs.

Furthermore, major businesses are now moving much of their work load to employees who labor at home computers, connected to the main office by modem. These employees don't even drive to work; they simply do their jobs at home and send in the results by means of a computer.

Of course, there will probably always be a place in the work force for part-timers who want to work at careers such as hairstyling and cosmetology, dental, medical, and library assisting, secretarial work, part-time teaching, retail selling, day-care and baby-sitting services, and party-plan sales. Many of these part-time or home careers allow you the luxury of choosing your own work schedule and deciding how much time and energy you wish to devote to the job.

Sure, there are trade-offs and drawbacks to part-time employment for moms; but you must weigh those against the disastrous price tag of drug addiction, emotional maladjustment, or a host of other plagues upon our society that are often the result of children being abused or neglected by stretched-out, stressed-out parents. Ask yourself this tough question: "How much am I willing to sacrifice in order to create a home environment that is conducive to the physical, emotional, intellectual, and spiritual growth of our family?"

If Mom Must Moonlight

Sometimes, despite every other effort, a mother working outside the home is absolutely unavoidable. In such cases, here are some practical suggestions that will help:

1. *Discuss your work with your child.* You don't need to dwell on all the details, but in a general way, describe to your child where it is you disappear to every day and what it is you do while you are there. Even a little knowledge about your job will help your child feel less abandoned and more secure. A succinct description is all that is necessary: "Daddy helps build homes for people" or "Mommy helps

people who are sick to feel better." Some jobs are more difficult to describe than others. When discussing what their fathers did for a living, my brother's ten-year-old son revealed to his friends, "My dad doesn't work; he's a preacher."

2. *Limit your work away from home if at all possible.* In contrast to my brother's son, another child in that group recounted sadly, "My mom works all the time. She leaves before I go to school in the morning and she doesn't get home until six o'clock at night. Dad makes supper, so we usually eat without Mom. She fixes something for herself, eats, does the dishes, and yells at us. She never seems to have time for anything else anymore."

Kids need parents who are there for them. Don't believe the myth that says, "Quality of time makes up for quantity of time." Kids don't know the difference. In fact, I have found that my daughter, Ashleigh, needs me to be available to her at some of the most inopportune times. How ludicrous it would be for me to say, "Sorry, honey. Daddy doesn't have time for you right now, but don't worry; we'll have some *quality* time whenever I get home." It has often been said, and needs to be said again and again, "Kids spell *love*: T-I-M-E." Make sure your work schedule allows for enough time to let your children know you love them and care about them.

3. *Keep your attitude and comments about your work on the positive side.* Even if your job is drudgery, your kids don't need to hear it. Certainly, you should teach them about the duties, frustrations, and responsibilities that work in the "outside world" requires, but leave the garbage on the job. Don't bring it home and dump it on your kids. They

need your comfort and attention, not your chronic complaints about your career.

If you have a bad day at work, try to unwind before you get home. Drive around the block a few extra times. Go jogging or do some other physical exercise. Take a hot shower as soon as you get in the house. Do whatever works to rid yourself of the negative feelings, but don't come home griping and grumping like Oscar the Grouch. Give yourself a chance to relax before plunging into your parenting responsibilities.

The attitude and work ethic your children develop will depend to a large degree on what they see and hear in you. Let them know when something good happens at work. Let them learn about the satisfaction and rewards that excellent work can bring. When your kids see you smiling about a job well done, a project completed, or some similar achievement, they will begin to understand and acquire a positive attitude toward work. On the other hand, if all they ever hear is how awful it is on the job, don't expect them to be scouring the "Help Wanted" ads.

4. *Limit any unnecessary nights away from home.* Whether for business, leisure, or church activities, don't allow your schedule to be so crammed that there is no time remaining for your children. If Mom must work outside the home, the kids may already feel cheated in the time department. Don't make them ask, "Why do my parents have to go out so much?"

I hear a familiar refrain from kids almost everywhere I travel to speak. It sounds like this: "My folks have time for everybody and everything but me." Ironically, preachers'

kids and children of parents involved in Christian minis-
tries are often among the most neglected.

If you attend a thriving church, you could easily be away
from home five or six evenings each week. Don't do it!
Certainly, you want to take advantage of spiritual-growth
opportunities, but you must limit your time away from
your family—especially if you are working outside the
home. Look at this lament and see if it sounds familiar:

> Mom works all day, five days a week. On Monday
> night she goes to choir practice. On Tuesday, she
> helps with the youth group. Wednesday night is Bi-
> ble study. Thursday, she plays on the church volley-
> ball team. Friday night, she and Dad go out or else
> they have friends over. There's always something go-
> ing on Saturday nights, and Sunday morning and
> evening, we have church. I feel almost as though
> Mom and Dad love church activities more than they
> love me!

Check your schedule and make sure you have enough
time to have dinner with the family, talk about important
matters, help with homework, or just spend a fun evening
together. Remember, what seems to you like a little bit of
time away from home may seem like an eternity to your
family. As a general rule, if you are out unnecessarily
more than one night per week, your kids probably feel
you are gone too much. Ask them to tell you honestly how
they feel about your absences. You may be surprised.

5. *Discipline yourself to listen to your children.* You expect
your kids to listen whenever you speak; unfortunately,
many parents do not give their children the same respect.

Again, if Mom is working outside the home, already your ideal listening opportunities are going to be limited, especially if you are not at home when the kids come in from school. You must compensate. You cannot afford to miss the chance to hear with your heart as well as with your ears.

What do most kids want to talk about? Their *feelings*. What do most parents want to talk about? The *facts*. Working moms are often too frazzled and frayed themselves to deal adequately with their children's feelings. Their attitude is, "Hey, just do what I told you," an answer that only in extremely rare instances has ever proven satisfactory to a child.

"Criticize your child less and listen more" is a good guide. If you don't listen to your kids, you will lose them. If you take the time to allow your children to truly communicate with you, even after a hard day's work, you can strengthen your relationship with them enormously.

6. *Start every day possible with prayer together.* You don't need to pray every morning for all the missionaries around the world (although praying for one or two specifically each day might be feasible), nor do you need to sing the doxology. Just take time to pray a simple prayer together as a family. You will be amazed how such a seemingly insignificant amount of prayer will help set a positive tone for your day. And don't be surprised when you see God's answers to those prayers!

In most homes, the family altar, that special place depicted in Sunday-school papers of yesteryear, where Mom, Dad, and the children used to read the Bible and pray together before going off to work or school, is practically a physical impossibility nowadays, especially for families with working moms.

"A 'quiet time,' " laughed Lori, a junior in high school. "That's a joke around our house. Our place is somewhere between a zoo and a traffic jam every morning. Everyone is running around screaming that they are going to be late. Mom and Dad are yelling at us: 'Hurry up in the bathroom! Brush your teeth. Eat your breakfast. *Then* brush your teeth. No, you can't wear that to school. Honey, where are my car keys?' It's crazy! I can't wait to get to school every day, just to clear my head."

Your mornings may be similar. It doesn't have to be that way, though. Try getting out of bed a few minutes earlier and slowing the pace a little. If at all possible, eat breakfast together as a family. It may be the last time you see each other until evening, so why not make the best of it? A few kind words of encouragement and a hug or a kiss before the family goes out the door will also work wonders.

7. *Provide for your children's safety.* If your kids must be home alone before or after school because both Mom and Dad are working, you need to exercise special precautions. Make sure your house is equipped with smoke detectors. A security system might be reassuring, provided your child knows how to arm and disarm it without unleashing the "Wrath of Khan" and the "Emergency Broadcast System."

If your child is not mature enough to carry a house key, leave one with a neighbor you can trust. Don't leave your doors unlocked all day and don't put a key under a doormat, above a ledge, or in any other obvious hiding place. Crooks have kids, too, you know.

If you are able to do so, call home as soon as possible

after your children have arrived from school. Just knowing you are thinking about them will give your kids a boost in their confidence level. Of course, this is also a great time for any afterschool instructions that might have been overlooked earlier in the day. Always post phone numbers where you and your spouse can be reached in an emergency.

Teach your children how to answer the telephone without letting a caller know that nobody else is at home. Some parents prefer to install telephone-answering machines. They instruct their kids to answer only when they hear a family member's voice on the machine's monitoring system.

Whatever you do, make sure everybody knows the rules about what is to be done during those "latchkey" hours. Spelling out specific instructions will give both you and your kids more security and greater peace of mind.

8. *Pray before bedtime.* Perhaps one of the most important habits a working mom can establish is the practice of praying with each child before bedtime. Certainly, this is an excellent regimen for all parents (Dad should join in, too), but this prayer time is essential when Mom has been away from the home all day. Nothing can replace a mother's prayers for her children.

Oh, sure, the kids may laugh, scoff, get embarrassed, and say, "Oh, Mom!" But they will remember those sessions for the rest of their lives. They will probably not remember the amount of your paycheck, but your investment of prayer in their lives will never be forgotten.

Moonlighting is never easy, but when it must be done, I believe God will give you the grace and the strength to balance your life-style. Difficult choices between what is good and what is best will constantly confront you, but with careful, prayerful attention to each other's needs, your marriage, your parenting responsibilities, and your career can work together.

One area that is extremely vulnerable to neglect, whether or not you are moonlighting, is your sexual relationship with your marriage partner. Now that's a subject worth considering. . . .

9
Strictly Confidential

Marriage Myth Number Eight:
The majority of your marriage will be spent in bed. Or,
"Fantasy Island, here we come!"

"The only people who make love all the time are
liars."

Louis Jordan

● ● ● ● ● ● ● ● ● ● ● ● ●

Go ahead. Flip through the channels on your television
some afternoon or evening. Almost anywhere you pause
long enough to peruse the programming, sensual images
will steam up your screen. Half-naked couples are cavort-
ing across your set, saying words and doing things that
only a few years ago would have landed them in prison
and branded you a pornographer for watching. "Sexual
realism," they call it.

Tune in any afternoon or evening "soap" or any "made
for TV" movie, or rent almost any video deemed more adult
than *Bambi,* and you will be exposed to couples playing
"bedfrog," a contemporary twist on an old-fashioned
game. If you were to believe what you see on the screen,
you could easily assume that most modern couples spend

years at a time in bed, kissing, cuddling, and caressing each other in continuous, if not contorted, ecstatic lovemaking. Don't those couples ever have to get up and go to work?

Normally, during a sixty-minute program or a ninety-minute movie, it takes about three minutes of mindless banter between a man and a woman to establish the intimate relationship described above. Miniseries relationships sometimes take longer, but you usually know before the credits roll on the first installment who is going to be bedding down with whom.

Now, I hate to be the one to burst your bubble, but . . . are you ready? Real life just isn't that way! Even the most amorous couples don't spend the majority of their time together in bed.

Of course, we all know that. Don't we? That mush we see on TV or in the movies or hear about in songs on the radio is the fiber they put in stuffed animals, isn't it? Fantasyland. A dream. Just an escape from reality.

Yet, knowing this full well, many modern couples have maintained the myth that their love lives will be one long string of romantic, sexually satisfying interludes, occasionally punctuated by mundane activities such as making a living, changing a diaper, or going to the dentist. As in so many other areas of marriage, when real life pinches at their idealism, couples often feel cheated.

"I honestly thought we'd have sex every single day or night," confessed a stunning newlywed in her mid-twenties. "I was surprised when, after we returned from our honeymoon and we both went back to work, we had relations only three or four times in a week."

Poor, deprived woman. I know married couples who would almost kill for her situation.

The frequency with which they have sexual intercourse is often a source of contention for a couple. Much of the confusion is created by the misconceptions and expectations each partner brings to the marriage. Sometimes it is just a matter of perspective. In the movie *Annie Hall*, the characters played by Woody Allen and Diane Keaton are shown simultaneously lamenting about their sex life to their therapists. She complains, "He wants sex all the time. At least four times a week." On a split screen, he tells the doctor they almost never have sex: "Four times a week at most."

Besides the "we'll have sex every night" delusion, other myths abound about sex in marriage. Perhaps the most preposterous proposition is that "super sex just happens naturally." Maybe so for dogs, cats, giraffes, elephants, birds, and bees, but not for you or me. For us, sexual intercourse is a learned activity. Oh, sure, any nominally normal man and woman can have sex; animal instinct can take you that far. But to experience the joys and intimacies of marital lovemaking that God intended when He dreamed up the whole idea will take some work. In that sense, making love is a complicated activity involving the total interaction of two people emotionally, physically, mentally, and—more than you may ever dream—spiritually.

Our society places a great deal of emphasis upon sexuality these days. You have the dubious distinction of being a part of the most sexually literate people ever to grace the face of the earth. You have been inundated with information about sex.

Unfortunately, in this sexually informed culture, you are bombarded by a horrendous amount of misinformation about sex. Consequently, most marriage partners begin their sex lives together with their minds muddled by sexual myths and misconceptions. For most modern couples, "fitting together" sexually is a process that may require as much "unlearning" as it does acquiring and assimilating correct information. Contrary to all the locker-room tales and coffee-klatch capers you have heard, there are no natural-born experts when it comes to sex. Furthermore, few couples are as sexually satisfied as they would like to be.

This is true despite the fact that, as a rule, contemporary men and women are more knowledgeable about sex than ever before and, due to the AIDS epidemic and other physically and emotionally devastating effects of the "sexual revolution," couples are more committed to monogamous relationships than in recent history.

Part of the explanation for this curious enigma might be "information overkill." We see and hear so much about sex, it is difficult to sort out the true from the false. For example, one of the strange behavior patterns spawned by the plethora of sexual stimuli and statistics around us is that many marriage partners now gauge their sex lives according to what they see and hear from other, often questionable, sources. They evaluate their most intimate relationships based on the latest gibberish spouted on "Geraldo," "Donahue," or some other talk show—rating everything from sexual techniques and positions, frequency of intercourse, length of time involved in sexual activity, to a host of other "criteria." Inevitably, even the most happily married couples begin to wonder, "Gee, maybe we aren't doing so well."

One fellow commented ruefully, "I feel as if every time we make love, my wife is going to hold up a series of cards with numbers on them, the way they do in the Olympics. 'Technique—seven.' 'Level of difficulty—five.' 'Overall effect—six.' I can't compete with the stuff she watches on TV."

The Sexless Marriage

One of the oddest and most tragic results of the sexual revolution has been what counselors are referring to as "inhibited sexual desire." Many married couples are living in the same house together, sleeping in the same bed, but not engaging in normal sexual intimacies. The problem is plaguing Christian couples as well as nonbelievers.

Curiously, this diminishing of sexual desire is not limited to the elderly. On the contrary, it is emerging in two groups supposedly notorious for their sexual passion and prowess: the baby boomers, men and women between thirty-five and forty-five years of age, and the Yuppies, well-educated men and women in their twenties or thirties.

What has caused this sexual sluggishness? Why are so many contemporary couples' sexual batteries in need of a supercharge? At least four reasons are worth considering.

First, as I have already mentioned, many men and women have been "desexualized" by media information overkill. Accurate or not, nowadays, many marriage partners feel they have seen it all, and many of them believe they have done it all. A forty-one-year-old woman offered this sad comment on the "new" morality: "I've had saturation sex since I was sixteen. I've tried everything anybody has suggested . . . and I've never found any real satisfaction." For the generation raised on the Rolling

Stones, Mick Jagger's monotonous message may have been prophetic: "I can't get no satisfaction."

The sexual mystique has been shattered. It is difficult to titillate a turned-off society. As one wry commentator put it, "We've gone from sex, drugs, and rock 'n' roll to celibacy, yogurt, and a VCR."

The second reason for the sexual complacency among many couples is a corollary to the first. Merely having seen and done it all does not quench one's thirst for new methods of sexual stimulation. Thus, we have witnessed the staggering proliferation of pornographic films and magazines. Although exact figures are understandably difficult to obtain, it is clear that much of the truly trashy material is being purchased by married individuals who satisfy themselves through masturbation rather than making love to their spouses. Currently, married men are the greatest offenders in this area, but the increasing sales of hard-core and soft-core materials to women may signal troubling times ahead for both genders.

A third reason for diminished sexual desire may be unique to our generation. While in the past men and women lusted for both sex and power, the baby boomers and the Yuppies are more obsessed with their careers than they are with sexual conquests. Certainly, they will take a bit of sex on the side if they can get it, but the real objects of their lust today are money, position, and prestige. Sadly, this is sublimation gone sour.

A fourth reason, to which I have already alluded, is that sexual performance has become paramount for many couples. Unfortunately, the new emphasis upon performance has caused many marriage partners to become so self-conscious about their "abilities" that they have become sexually disenchanted, and some even sexually dysfunctional. Consequently, counselors are constantly encountering what they call "the new impotence," caused primarily by the fact that partners have become so concerned about performance that they have begun to experience difficulties in their sexual relationship. Women feel cheated and men feel resentful, resulting in even less sexual desire.

It is ironic that many of those who shucked off God's commands concerning sex, and who helped launch the sexual revolution of the sixties and seventies, are now caught in its backlash. Then again, it's not so strange after all. Sin always has social ramifications. Some just take a little longer to seep into society's mainstream.

Isn't a Drop-off in Sex Normal?

Yes . . . and no. True, most couples experience a decrease in the frequency of sexual relations after the initial burst of sexual activity during the early days of their marriage. As a couple settles into their relationship, they feel more secure, less frenzied, and thus are able to establish a more comfortable, although less frequent, sexual schedule. That is normal.

A complete loss of sexual passion, however, is abnormal. Certainly, marriage tends to make sex more routine; the day-to-day intimate contact and accessibility sometimes tarnishes the sexual luster in a relationship. Nitty-gritty responsibilities of marriage also take a toll. Dealing with mundane household chores and paying monthly bills are not nearly as exciting as the dinner and walk along a moonlit beach you enjoyed before you were married.

Unquestionably, tension or unresolved conflict in your relationship will diminish sexual desire; stress, anxiety, fatigue, and exhaustion will almost always cause desire to dwindle.

When sexual passion dissipates, it casts a pall over an entire relationship. Maria's husband, Bob, has already been through several mid-life crises, and he is only in his early forties. The couple has one child, but the chances of their having another are remote, even though Maria, who is younger than Bob, is still in her childbearing years. Maria and Bob have not had sexual relations in over two years.

Bob is a respected engineer at a nuclear energy plant and a leader in his local church. He pours himself into his work, his child, and his altruistic activities, all done in the Name of the Lord.

While Maria is not totally disconsolate about their relationship, she is concerned:

> We have a beautiful home, a nice car, lovely things, and a child we both adore. But I do worry about Bob not wanting me. Sometimes I let my imagination run wild and I start thinking he is having an affair with someone else, but I don't think that is the case. Maybe part of it is my fault. But what can I do?

What Can We Do to Improve Our Sex Lives?

In his excellent book *Love Life for Every Married Couple*, Dr. Ed Wheat pinpoints three areas that must be concentrated upon if you hope to improve your sexual relationship with your mate:

169

1. You must acquire *correct* medical information about sex.
2. You must establish a biblical understanding of the sexual relationship.
3. You must develop and practice a *proper* approach to lovemaking within your marriage.

First, to help you acquire correct medical information, along with a Christian perspective and appreciation for God's great gift of your sexuality, I highly recommend Dr. Wheat's well-known work *Intended for Pleasure* (Revell, 1981). As a Christian medical doctor, Wheat provides a wealth of understandable, practical information about how you and your mate can enjoy your sexual relationship more fully, while solving or avoiding some of the most common sexual problems in marriage. Don't assume that you know enough about sex already, and don't allow pride to keep you from better understanding the physical aspect of your relationship. Remember, much of what we have learned about sex is based upon myth and misinformation. You need dependable, accurate facts if you want to improve your sex life.

Second, you must establish a biblical attitude toward sexuality. I cannot overemphasize that you need an accurate understanding of what the Bible *says*, not what people say the Bible *means*, no matter how well intentioned or ill intentioned their motives. Nowadays, it is common for Christians to be caricatured as holding to some warped, Victorian, or puritanical view of sex. Nothing could be further from the truth.

If you actually study the Bible, you will discover that it was God who created your sexuality; He gave you your sexual organs and your sexual desires, and He has declared them "good." It is not sexuality that God condemns but sexual *immorality*. The Scripture is consistent in its message: "Let marriage be held in honor among all, and let the marriage bed be undefiled; for fornicators and adulterers God will judge" (Hebrews 13:4). The word translated "bed" in the verse is actually the word *coitus* in Greek, a word meaning sexual intercourse. The word *undefiled* means "not sinful, not dirty or soiled in any way." Clearly the writer is saying, "Sex within marriage is honorable; it is not dirty in the least."

Sadly, some Christians have been confused or misled at this point. Strange as it may seem, certain ascetic teachers still assert that sex is something to be endured rather than enjoyed. This is an unbiblical teaching and should be rejected. It is totally inconsistent with God's Word.

In fact, the Bible makes it clear that a husband and wife should meet each other's needs by *regularly* engaging in sexual intercourse. When a group of misguided believers began to think and do otherwise, the Apostle Paul firmly rebuked them:

> Let the husband fulfill his duty to his wife, and likewise also the wife to her husband. The wife does not have authority over her own body, but the husband does; and likewise also the husband does not have authority over his own body, but the wife does. Stop depriving one another, except by agreement for a time that you may devote yourselves to prayer, and come together again lest Satan tempt you because of your lack of self-control.
>
> 1 Corinthians 7:3–5

Paul is saying that a married couple should do everything they can to meet each other's sexual needs. This principle is not only a fundamental part of marriage but it is also protection against temptations the devil may hurl at a couple who do not regularly participate in sexual intimacies—temptations such as immorality, lust, and evil thoughts, to be sure, but also temptations toward bitterness, anger, jealousy, envy, malice, and strife.

Paul puts it bluntly and Christian husbands and wives need to understand this important principle: *Your spiritual life is intimately related to your sex life!* If you are out of whack spiritually, your sexual relationship with your spouse is going to be affected. If you are married and you are not engaging in normal, regular sexual relations (barring disability or limited, brief periods of abstinence in order to pray, as Paul describes), your spiritual life is bound to be impacted negatively. God intended for married men and women to enjoy their sexual relationship throughout their marriage, far beyond their childbearing years.

Don't allow yourself to be deluded into thinking that sex does not matter. Granted, while sex is not everything, or even the main thing, in a good relationship, it is *something!*

If you are married and are not sexually active with your spouse, do not ignore the situation. You may need medical help. Professional Christian counseling may be beneficial for both you and your mate. Perhaps, though, the problem may be solved simply by clearing out the rubble of past misinformation and developing a biblical approach to sex.

Regardless of where you acquired the misinformation that haunts your mind—through a poor parental example, a distorted sex education at home or in school, an abusive or otherwise negative sexual experience as a child, premarital sex, a homosexual or adulterous relationship, or simply an unfulfilled sexual history in marriage—if you will establish a proper biblical attitude toward sex, the truth will set you free (John 8:31, 32).

How to Develop a Proper Approach

I am not a clinical psychologist, nor am I a modern-day "sexpert," so I will refrain from commenting upon such matters as the proper positions in which to place your hands and feet during foreplay, or the sexual inhibitions of Pygmies. I'll gladly leave the technical discussion of terms and techniques to those more qualified than I. The principles I share here, however, have been tried and proven by multitudes of marriage partners with whom I have counseled and shared advice over the past twenty years. These suggestions are not meant to be a substitute for technical information but a supplement to it.

You must deal radically and realistically with sexual myths. Many of these myths have to do with male attitudes toward sex. For example, a common misconception is that a man has a greater sex drive than a woman does. This leads to the familiar female charge, "All you ever think about is sex!" which is usually countered by the male retort, "Oh, yeah? Well, you *never* seem to think about sex. You ought to try it sometime—you might like it!"

At this point, couples frequently begin commenting upon each other's anatomies or parentage and the discussion rapidly degenerates (as does the relationship).

The truth is, men do *not* have a greater sex drive than women. It may seem that men are more interested in sex, but as modern women concur, that is a myth also. Nevertheless, men do tend to place a higher priority upon physical response than do most women. Men seek a physical expression of love before they can move on to the more emotional aspects of intimacy. Women, however, normally desire emotional intimacy before engaging in sexual expressions of intimacy. Most women desire romance, not merely sexual release.

Of course, men want and need romance, too. They just have a difficult time separating love and romance from sex.

This often leads to what I call the "Slam, Bang, Crash, Pop, Boom, Whish" approach to lovemaking. The husband rushes into the bedroom like the Lone Ranger on an impassioned mission, grabs his wife, makes mindless love, and is gone. Meanwhile, the stunned, unsatisfied wife is wondering, *Who* was *that masked man?*

Slow down, guys! You need to understand that your wife wants you to hold her, caress her, touch her tenderly, and make her feel like a woman of worth. While you might be ready to have sex at a moment's notice, your wife needs to be aroused emotionally as well as physically.

Noted author and lecturer Gary Smalley whimsically compares the difference between male and female sexual arousal to a microwave oven and a Crockpot. Smalley says most men are similar to microwave ovens; they can be turned on and fully activated almost instantaneously with only the press of a few buttons. Women, on the other hand, are more like Crockpots. They need time to simmer.

That usually takes some time, but it will be time well spent. For the husband who is willing to take the time to develop and practice the proper attitude and approach to lovemaking, the question of who has the greater sexual desire will become academic.

Understand, the intensity of a woman's sexual desire is no less than that of a man. Furthermore, these desires are not dirty, evil, or sinful, as long as they are expressed within the context of marriage. In this regard, many Christian women are only beginning to come out from under the covers. For years, Christian women have been shackled with the false notion that they should not enjoy or express their sexual desires, not even within marriage. Unfortunately, this attitude was often fostered by misinformed or misguided religious teachers. Sylvia and Joe, both devout Christians, almost lost their marriage because of the perpetuation of these destructive myths. Sylvia admitted:

> The way my mom and some of the other women in our church referred to sex, I was scared to death to even think about it. On our honeymoon, I cringed every time Joe touched me. I felt desires deep within me that I wanted to express, but because of my religious background, every time I tried to let go, I'd feel like a tramp; so I continued to hold back.
>
> Joe sensed my alienation and began to withdraw. We tried to talk about it, but I couldn't even speak the words. Whenever Joe's advances seemed unavoidable, I closed my eyes and tolerated it. But I never allowed myself to enjoy making love, if that's what you can call what we did.
>
> Before long, I began avoiding sexual contact with Joe any way I could. I'd go to bed before he did and pretend I was asleep. I'd get out of bed early and

make breakfast, just to keep from lying in bed together. I would never allow him to see me naked, and I tried not to look at his body. Something inside me kept saying, "This is weird. This is not the way marriage is meant to be," but I also kept hearing those voices from my youth describing sex in such terrible terms.

Finally, Joe couldn't take it anymore. He asked me for a divorce. I didn't know what else to do, so I called a pastor from another church in town. I didn't dare talk to *our* pastor about our problem. I felt he would condemn me for even thinking about sex, much less divorce!

The pastor from across town agreed to see me on one condition—that Joe come along. Joe said he would go.

That pastor began to teach us from the Bible about sex. At first, I was uncomfortable with what he was saying, but little by little, the Lord revealed the truth to me.

I asked Joe to forgive me for my foolishness. He understood that I really never intended to hurt him; I just didn't know how to deal with the intense desires I felt on the one hand and the attitudes I had adopted about sex on the other. We're still working on our relationship, and I have a long way to go; but we have started. Why didn't anyone ever tell me it was okay for a Christian woman to enjoy sex in her marriage?

Talking Is Not Always the Answer

Another myth concerning married sex that needs to be corrected says, "Any married couple can improve their sex lives by honest, frank communication about their sexual problems." If this myth were actually true, a large percentage of the divorce lawyers, psychologists, sexual clinicians, and talk-show hosts would be out of work.

Ideally, you should be able to communicate lovingly with your spouse about sexual needs and what he or she can do to make your lovemaking more pleasing. Ideally, you should be able to receive your spouse's constructive criticisms concerning your willingness to satisfy his or her sexual needs and preferences. Ideally.

Unfortunately, many couples are not nearly so adept at communicating about sex as they might think. Furthermore, if their communication lines were so open, loving, tender, compassionate, and unselfish, they probably would not be experiencing serious problems in the first place! Great sex begins in the head and in the heart, long before it ever stimulates the loins.

What often happens when couples attempt to communicate about their sexual needs or concerns is that they quickly slip into quagmires of guilt, blame, or criticism. It's tough to talk to your partner about how he or she is not meeting your needs without making your spouse feel like a total reject. Conversely, it is difficult to accept constructive criticism concerning your own sexual attitudes and techniques. Frequently, when couples dare to broach these subjects, somebody goes away feeling angry, hurt, bitter, inadequate, or disgusted—not exactly a prescription for improved sexual intimacy.

Please don't misinterpret my message. I am not advocating less communication about sex in marriage. You should and you *must* attempt to communicate honestly and openly about sex with your spouse. You will never improve your sexual relationship merely by gathering more information. You must find out what pleases your mate and you must impart to your partner a working understanding of what makes you tick sexually, too. Your mate will not be able to know your true needs, desires, and feelings if you clam up and don't express yourself. It is almost impossible to solve a sexual problem if one or both refuses to acknowledge its existence.

Nevertheless, you need to be extremely sensitive when you discuss sexual dissatisfaction. Sexual egos are fragile; they bruise easily.

Dozens of fine books, written from a Christian perspective, include lists of suggestions how a husband and wife can make their sexual relationship more meaningful. This information may be helpful to you. My only caution concerning these lists is this: Most men do not enjoy discussing them with their wives! Although men can be extremely list-orientated in other areas (for example: business, sports standings, or financial goals), most men do not appreciate running through a checklist on their sex lives.

Perhaps a better approach might be for you and your partner to read those helpful materials individually and then, when both of you are in the mood to discuss the subject (when you are not tired, wet, or hungry!), ask the question, "Honey, on a scale of one to a thousand, how would you rate our sex life?" Of course, a scale of one to ten will serve adequately, but sports-orientated guys are often comforted by the fact that nobody bats one thousand, and a baseball player is considered a stellar success if he gets a hit during one-third of his attempts at bat.

Whatever scale you choose to use, giving your relationship a number will at least set you up for the more important follow-up question: "How could I help to raise that number?"

At this point, if you are the partner who is asking the question, you can draw from the reservoir of information and suggestions you have read and you could say, "Well, dear, if you would wear something besides asbestos pajamas to bed, that might raise the number a few notches." Well, maybe not.

"Take a shower before coming to bed."

"Touch me and caress me."

"Talk to me before, during, and after intercourse."

"Let me know what you enjoy rather than complaining about what you dislike."

The list could go on and on, but I'm sure you have the idea. The important thing is to take advantage of the opportunity to hear your partner and to express your own sexual needs. Don't get bogged down or overwhelmed. ("Yes, George. Now that you asked, here is a computer printout of sixty-two areas in which you could improve your lovemaking skills.") Talk about only a few items at a time, and then attempt to respond to your partner's suggestions the next time you make love. Maintain a lighthearted attitude during your discussion. Remember, those sensitive egos need encouragement, not criticism. Don't be afraid to show your honest surprise and interest when your mate reveals a desire or need to you: "Really? You want me to touch you like that? Okay, great!" Or, "I'm not quite sure I understand what you mean. Here, take my hand and show me." You may feel a bit foolish at first, but your mate will appreciate your sincere desire to improve your sexual relationship.

179

More Practical Tips to Improve Your Sexual Relationship

1. *Turn off the television.* The TV has ruined the sex lives of more contemporary couples than any other culprit. It is an intruder, a disrupter, a robber—and I'm not even considering the *content* of contemporary programs. I'm talking about the *time* it steals from your relationship.

In a *Redbook* magazine article (July 1986), author Nina Combs suggests that multitudes of modern couples are allowing their sex lives to literally slip down "the tube." She implies that the magic button to put joy back into your marriage might well be the "off" switch on your TV set.

In Combs' article, Pierre Mornell, a California psychologist, cautions, "If you're watching more than an hour or two a night, you could be more tuned into TV than you are to each other."

When I mentioned this during a marriage seminar at which I was speaking, one woman whispered much too loudly to her husband, "I bet we could improve our sex life seventy-five percent if you'd just shut that television off and go to bed with me at a decent hour!" Titters from those who overheard her remark caused me to conclude that several other women in the room shared her sentiments. Another woman blurted out, "Amen, sister. Preach it!"

If you have a television in the bedroom, you must meticulously legislate its intrusion. The danger is not the actions television produces but the actions it prevents. By turning off the TV, you may have a much better chance of turning each other on. If you discover you cannot or will not discipline yourselves in regard to bedroom TV viewing, remove the set from the room before it robs you of your sexual relationship.

2. *Remember, great sex starts long before you take clothes off.* Often, an evening of ecstasy may be triggered (or squelched) by the way you treat each other early in the morning. For example, a husband kisses his wife as he or she goes out the door for work in the morning and then mischievously adds, "I can't wait to be home with you tonight. We're going to try out our new bathtub Jacuzzi."

"But honey, we don't *have* a Jacuzzi."

"I know," he replies with a grin.

That sort of exchange might create immeasurable anticipation . . . of course, it might also get you committed to an asylum. Nevertheless, compare that patter to this: On the way out the door, you say, "Oh, boy. I know this is going to be a long, tough day. The boss wants me to work overtime, and I've got to stop at the dry cleaner, the grocery store, and the service station after work. I'll probably be late tonight and exhausted when I get home." If you leave your mate with that discouraging list, don't be surprised when the sexual signals in his or her eyes shift from bright green to dull yellow to an emphatic red. Nobody looks forward to another evening of whining about how tired you are. Avoid complaints and criticism altogether, and you will stand a much better chance of improving your sexual relationship.

Speak positive words of affirmation, appreciation, and anticipation, and start early in the day. Then, if possible, reinforce those words throughout the day, perhaps with a surprise phone call or a special card. Give each other romantic caresses at times when you both know that sex is an impossibility, or at least highly unlikely! Affectionate words, glances, and touches will all tend to heighten your sexual desire for each other.

Sexual intimacy cannot be created instantly; you cannot turn on your spouse's desire the way you would a light switch. Great sex demands an investment of time, encouragement, and nourishment of your entire relationship. If there is stress or strain in other areas of your marriage, it is bound to show up in your sex life. In other words, what goes on between the two of you *outside* the bedroom will make or break you between the sheets.

Men, especially, need to be reminded of this truth. Many guys feel that any problem in marriage can be cured by jumping into bed. The exact opposite is true. If there is a problem somewhere else in the relationship, sex is the furthest thing from the minds of most women.

"Date your mate" if you want to keep sex exciting or make your relationship more thrilling. Sadly, after a few years of marriage, many marriage partners quit doing the things that made them so irresistible to their mates during dating days. A leisurely walk in the park, flowers for no specific reason, that favorite fragrance, love songs and poetry, hugs, kisses, holding hands, eye-to-eye contact when talking, cards, or unexpected little gifts are all ways of nourishing passion.

Angela and I have a special ritual that holds a strange romantic power for us. Occasionally, one of us will call the other by phone and immediately, without a word of greeting, launch into the chorus of Stevie Wonder's hit song, "I Just Called to Say I Love You." Whoever received the call joins right in singing along.

What is so strange about that? you may be wondering.

We sing it as though we are drunk—and we don't drink!

I've often wondered what kind of impression we are making upon any operator who might be listening, but that hasn't kept us from sharing our pseudoinebriated love song. Hey, I didn't say it was normal! I just said it is special to us.

Tender gestures of love or thoughtfulness that were special to you during your dating days, or any loving expressions you have developed since marrying, will enhance your partner's desire. Take those extra pains to treat your mate the way you did when the two of you were dating, and then watch out as you see your relationship revive.

3. *Be creative*. One of the most serious threats to your sex life is not competition from a younger or better lover but boredom on the part of you or your spouse. In fact, one of the main causes of sexual affairs is sexual boredom.

Don't allow your lovemaking to become dull, monotonous, or routine. Understand: it is *your* responsibility, not your mate's, to keep your sex life exciting.

An irate man in his mid-forties accosted me at a marriage seminar where I was speaking. "Be creative. *Be creative;* that's all I ever hear from you guys who teach these seminars. Be creative. And I hate it!"

"Why is that, sir?" I asked in my best Detective Joe Friday voice.

"Because I'm *not* creative!" he shouted. "Furthermore, I don't know *how* to be creative, and I'm not sure I'd *want* to be creative if I did know how!"

He is not alone. For many men, the idea of being a creative lover conjures up images of some twerp who sits cross-legged on the beach, stares at the stars, and croons love songs to the moon. Most guys just don't see themselves in that picture.

When I say to be creative in your love life, I don't intend for you to be artistic, clever, or even poetic. Nor am I recommending that you experiment with the variety of wild, contorted sexual positions being advocated today. You needn't be a gymnast to be a creative lover. All you need is a little ingenuity. Be a bit unpredictable. Try something different once in a while! Don't allow your lovemaking to become dull.

Committed Christian couples may be especially susceptible to boredom in the bedroom. After all, it takes quite a bit of creativity to be able to make love with the same person for fifty or sixty years and still keep the relationship exciting.

"Exciting?" quipped one senior citizen. "I'd be happy if she'd just stay awake during intercourse!"

Sleeping habits notwithstanding, you can keep your sex life new and refreshing, even after years of marriage. Try engaging in sexual relations at an unusual time or in a room other than the bedroom. Have you ever made love under the Christmas tree? In the bathroom? On your lunch hour? Under the kitchen table? *On* the kitchen table? Okay, you have the idea.

Perhaps a minivacation would add some zest to your relationship. Have you ever noticed that you and your spouse seem to enjoy sex more while on vacation? It's not just the air. Part of the enchantment comes from a new location. Obviously, you cannot go on vacation every month, but you can do *something* to break out of the regular routine. An evening together away from home, for example, may help breathe some fresh air into a stale love life. Where you go and what you do is not nearly so important as fracturing those old, familiar response patterns.

Certainly, some of the old standbys are still effective: candlelight dinners, flowers, sexy lingerie, and other "aphrodisiacs" can help rekindle a waning sexual flame. Perhaps one of the most creative stimulants to your sex life might be sending the kids to Grandma and Grandpa's for the night!

4. *Be realistic in your sexual expectations.* If you expect fireworks, flashing lights, and marching bands every time you make love, you are going to be deeply disappointed in your mate and in yourself. Sure, ecstasy is possible every time you have sex, but it is not necessary. It is equally important for you and your partner simply to come together in mutually satisfying physical closeness. Whether or not you experience an ecstatic orgasm is irrelevant. As Dr. Ed Wheat has observed in *Love Life for Every Married Couple*, "When couples strive to obtain an orgasm without regard to enjoying their time together, sex becomes work rather than pleasure. Remember that orgasm lasts only a few seconds. Emotional satisfaction and gratification occur during the entire episode."

5. *Have fun with sex.* Certainly, the sexual relationship is a serious and sacred aspect of your marriage, but many couples take sex so seriously, they miss one of the main fringe benefits: fun! Remember, God did not create sex only for procreation but also for a married couple's recreation.

Sometimes your sexual encounters with your spouse may be passionate and romantic; at other times they may be intense and frenzied. But don't miss the joy of just having fun with sex. Do something silly or spontaneous. Don't be afraid to laugh and have lighthearted fun while making love with the partner God has given you.

Real Life Isn't So Bad

Okay, maybe you won't make wild, passionate, ecstatic love every night of your marriage. But in a loving, Christ-centered marriage, the oneness, intimacy, and love you share far exceeds in quality what the Hollywood myth makers attempt to palm off as possible through sheer quantity of encounters. This is definitely one area in marriage where *quality* is more important than *quantity*.

Granted, the longer you are married, the less you may have of those heartthrobbing, breathless, palm-sweating sexual experiences you had in the early days of your relationship; but you will have more security, a deepening of your love and commitment to each other, and an awesome appreciation for the God who created the exciting, mysterious gift of your sexuality.

Married sex may or may not be as erotically exciting as the myth makers say sex with a stranger is supposed to be, but sex with a stranger can never provide the deep, fulfilling satisfaction that comes to two lovers whose union is blessed by the God of all creation.

10
The Most Dangerous Myth of Marriage

Marriage Myth Number Nine:
An affair could never happen to me. Or, "We love each other! We wouldn't think of taking one another for granted."

"No good Christian man or woman gets up in the morning, looks out the window, and says, 'My, this is a lovely day! I guess I'll go out and commit adultery.' Yet many do it anyway."

Florence Littauer

• • • • • • • • • • • • • •

She was gorgeous. As the tall, slender beauty entered the room, the eyes of the other seminar participants automatically gravitated toward her. She carried herself with an air of sophistication and class that family background and big bucks cannot buy. Yet, as she took a seat near the front, I noticed that her eyes betrayed a sadness deep within.

My topic for the one-day, single-parent seminar was "The Walking Wounded: Divorce Is Not the Unpardonable Sin." As I began my talk, I wondered how the subject matter applied to the svelte woman in the second row. After the session, I found out.

Her name was Nicolette, and she and her husband, Tom, had been married for fourteen years before Nicolette discovered Tom was having an affair with another woman. Both Nicolette and Tom were Christians. Their story could have been scripted for a soap opera, but the trace of tears that misted Nicolette's eyes as she talked reminded me that this was an all-too-true tragedy.

They had been high school sweethearts, so nobody was surprised when they married before Tom had completed his first year of college. Shortly after the wedding, Nicolette quit college and went to work selling pharmaceuticals while Tom went on with his education. Nicolette worked hard to help pay Tom's way through his undergraduate studies and then even harder to see him through law school. It was a sacrifice she was glad to make; she knew that Tom was going to become a great lawyer. And he did.

Along the way, Nicolette acquired a genuine interest in her career and quickly rose to a top-management position in a leading pharmaceuticals company. The couple was a perfect picture of a Christian baby-boomer success story.

Then, after twelve years of marriage, Nicolette gave birth to a son, Nathan. That's when the trouble started:

> I wasn't the one who wanted children in the first place. Tom was the one pressing for kids. I was quite content with our marriage, and I was happy pursuing my career. Looking back, I'm wondering if Tom's affair had not already begun and he may have thought that with a baby to take care of, I wouldn't notice his indiscretions as much. At the same time, in his academic way, he might have reasoned that a baby would be a surrogate love object for me, sort of a human teddy bear.
>
> Almost immediately after Nathan's birth, I began to notice changes in Tom's attitude toward me. He

didn't treat me badly or anything. In fact, he went overboard to help in every way he could. But the big change came in our sex life. After Nathan was born, Tom didn't want to touch me. He developed a kind of "Madonna Complex"; maybe he viewed me more as a mother than as his wife. Regardless, he began shying away from any sexual contact with me.

He began working late a lot and receiving quite a few strange "consultant" calls at home. Whenever I'd ask him about these things, he'd become verbally abusive. He never hit me, but on several occasions, I thought he might.

I knew something was up, so I hired a private detective to follow Tom to one of his emergency case briefings. Tom is an excellent lawyer, so I knew that before I accused him of anything, I'd better have positive proof. It wasn't long in coming. The detective brought back pictures and everything.

When I confronted Tom about the affair, he denied it vociferously. I said, "Tom, I've got pictures of you and her together right here!" He still denied it up and down. We went on like that for over an hour. Finally, he just looked at me and said, "Okay, what do you want?"

"I want *everything*," I said. "The house, a car, child support, the works. If you think you can just walk away after fourteen years of marriage, you'd better know there is a high cost." Unfortunately, his mind was already made up and price was no deterrent. Our divorce became final last week.

Then Nicolette said something counselors are hearing from Christian marriage partners with ever-increasing frequency. While her sad eyes blinked back the tears, Nicolette said quietly, "I don't know what happened. We were so happy—at least, I thought we were. I never dreamed an affair could happen to us."

Since When Have Affairs Become Cool?

Men have always been infamous for their marital infidelities. Recently, however, women have shown that "what's rotten for the goose can also be rotten for the gander."

For her book *The Cosmo Report* (Arbor, 1981), author Linda Wolfe surveyed 106,000 women. She discovered that of those women over the age of thirty-four, nearly 70 percent had indulged in at least one extramarital affair since being married.

It is understandable, almost expected, that a society which has bought into an existentialistic "do your own thing" philosophy of life would have few qualms about extramarital affairs. Secular humanists who believe man is god can hardly be blamed whenever they seek to satisfy their own self-interests; hedonists, those who regard pursuit of pleasure as the ultimate quest in life, surely cannot be required to remain faithful to a marriage partner, especially if that faithfulness impinges upon an individual's personal desires. Perhaps it is naive to ask immoral or amoral people to behave "properly"; people who have debunked any Absolute Authority or value system cannot be expected to honor personal commitment. Why should they?

We understand why flagrant, unrepentant sinners act sinfully. It's their nature! The tough question is this: How can Christians—men and women who claim to value fidelity so fastidiously, who believe in irrevocable commitments, and who bandy about such scathing rebukes of Judas-type betrayals—get caught up in extramarital affairs?

Part of the answer may lie in our contemporary, saccharine-sounding label: *affair*. It sounds so much nicer than adultery or the old King James descriptive term: *whoremongering*. Few Christian men or women would want to be branded adulterers or whoremongers, yet, while accurate statistics are difficult to obtain, surveys continue to reveal that the percentage of Christian men and women who are engaging in extramarital liaisons is almost identical to that of their non-Christian counterparts. Few contemporary Christians describe their "affairs" as sin. J. Allan Petersen keenly observes in *The Myth of the Greener Grass* (Tyndale, 1983), "What was once labeled adultery and carried a stigma of guilt and embarrassment now is an affair—a nice-sounding, almost inviting word wrapped in mystery, fascination, and excitement. A relationship, not sin."

Nevertheless, for all our semantics, one need not be a theologian to understand the seventh commandment: "Thou shalt not commit adultery" (Exodus 20:14 KJV). Furthermore, throughout the Scripture, God's wayward people were characterized as *adulterers*, and their disobedient actions always resulted in God's judgment and punishment of their sin. The implications are obvious, but for those who refuse to make the connection, the writer to the Hebrews spells it out specifically: "Fornicators and adulterers God will judge" (Hebrews 13:4). Call it what you will—an affair, a relationship, a liaison, a dalliance, a rendezvous, a fling, or any other socially acceptable term—

God calls any immoral indiscretions outside of marriage *sin*, with a capital *S*.

Or, as Linda Ellerbee adroitly declares in her book, *And So It Goes* (Berkley, 1987), "Dreck is dreck, and no amount of fancy polish will make it anything else." Whatever dreck is.

What Causes Sexual Affairs?

Ask anyone who has ever been involved in an immoral relationship why it happened, and you will always receive an answer. It may border on the absurd, but there is always a "reason" for the affair—at least in the minds of the offending parties.

Real or imagined, I have pinpointed six major "reasons" for extramarital affairs. I mention these not to condone the actions or to excuse the participants but to alert you to some of the danger signs and possibly prevent you from experiencing the awful pain that inevitably accompanies an immoral relationship.

1. *Sexual conquest.* While presumably not a predominant reason for Christians becoming involved in affairs, there are still plenty of men (and a rising number of women) who feel the only way they can stroke their self-image is by "conquering" another person. In marriage, where sex is more accessible, some husbands and wives discover that half the fun was the challenge. Consequently, temptation looms whenever another person appears on the scene as a potential conquest—a new challenge. Often, the person most susceptible to this type of affair is the one who has recently suffered some sort of setback in another area of his or her life.

Bill explained to me how this happened to him:

> I had been with my company for almost twenty years and was by far the most experienced guy in our sales force. But when my boss retired, the company passed me by and promoted a fellow with far less experience or expertise. I was hurt and disappointed. I guess it hit me that I had reached the pinnacle of my career and would probably advance no further.
>
> About that time, Betty was hired as the new sales coordinator. Part of my job required that I call in a report to her each afternoon, and somehow during one of our conversations, I allowed a double entendre to slip. Betty didn't respond positively . . . but she didn't react negatively, either. That was the start. From then on, it was a challenge. I began purposely peppering my reports each day with sexual overtones, subtly at first, then more blatantly. Always in good taste, of course, and with plenty of humor.
>
> I became obsessed with the idea of possessing the woman behind the voice on the phone. I was happily married to a loving wife, the father of two great kids. But our marriage had become stagnant, and I needed a new challenge. Betty was it.

Bill persistently pursued Betty for more than six months before he finally caught her. By then, their playful conversations each day had become the only bright spot in Bill's job. Had it not been for her, he probably would have quit, but he couldn't stop until he had succeeded in winning her affection. It wasn't love; it was conquest.

When Bill finally bedded down with Betty, their affair

was short-lived. Once he had "conquered" her, his ego assuaged, he no longer desired her. The consequences of his conquest, however, were costly. When Betty's supervisor overheard one of the lovers' "extracurricular" phone conversations on company time, she began monitoring their calls. She soon realized this was a regular pattern; subsequently, both Bill and Betty were fired. When the reason for their departure became known to the public, Bill's wife threw him out. Bill blamed Betty for not being more careful, and she broke off with him, too.

Silly as it may sound, the entire series of events transpired as a result of Bill's foolish attempt to boost his faltering self-esteem following his failure to receive a promotion.

Sexual conquest by women is also on the rise, perhaps a by-product of the shifting behavior patterns among modern men and women. In recent years more women have become openly aggressive about pursuing and conquering a male "sex object." While some may applaud this development as a giant step forward in the quest for equal rights, what it really amounts to is that we now have two genders using and abusing each other for their own gratification. Not exactly progress.

2. *Loneliness or lack of intimacy.* When the most important human being in your life is not interested in the details of your day or willing to share your triumphs and failures, your joys and sorrows, or even the minor events of your life, loneliness is the inevitable result.

Said Debbie, a sincere Christian woman and mother of a three-year-old:

> Stewart must travel for his business. I understand that part. But when he comes home, he brings stacks

of paperwork with him. What little time we have together is consumed by recuperating from his last trip or getting ready for the next one. We rarely share a relaxed, adult conversation anymore. Stewart receives immense mental stimulation and satisfaction from his job, but my deepest discussions have been on a three-year-old level.

I never intended to have an affair, but I was longing for somebody to talk to, somebody to share my world and to open me up to worlds beyond diapers and dishes. That's when my car broke down on the way home from the doctor's office. There I was, stuck alongside the road, with Mandy, our daughter. A fellow in a pickup truck stopped to offer assistance. I recognized him immediately. His name was Pete, and he lived down the road from us. He couldn't get the car going, so I gratefully accepted a ride home.

Mandy fussed all the way, but despite the distraction, Pete and I did something Stewart and I hadn't done in a long time: we *talked*. Nothing serious, but he showed a genuine interest in me. When we arrived home, I invited him in for coffee. He politely refused, shook my hand, and was on his way, but that was the beginning.

Our affair didn't happen overnight, the way you see things portrayed on TV. Pete drove by our house quite often and if I was outside, I'd always wave. He'd honk the horn of his pickup and smile. After awhile, I found myself looking for Pete's truck. Sometimes he'd stop, and if I was working in the yard, which I started doing a lot, he'd get out of his truck and we'd talk. That was it, just talk. We talked about everything and anything except diapers and dishes.

Then one night Mandy developed a dangerously high fever. Stewart was out of town, and I was frantic. I called Pete.

He came right over, and we raced Mandy to the hospital in Pete's pickup. We spent the entire night together in the emergency room. The doctor decided to admit Mandy, so at dawn, Pete drove me home. Exhausted and emotionally spent, we tumbled into bed together. We didn't even have sex that first time; we just held each other. Nevertheless, having a compassionate man—a man who really cared about Mandy and me—sleeping next to me filled me with more contentment than I had known in ages.

Pete is not particularly good-looking. He is not brilliant or rich, but he gives me something Stewart never has time to give me: himself.

3. *Boredom, monotony, and depression.* Where you find loneliness, you will usually find these three causes as well.

"Marriage just wasn't fun anymore," was Steve's excuse for an affair. "When we first married, Susan's and my relationship was exciting, happening, going places, doing things; we were passionately in love. Now our marriage is dry and dull. When one of the women in the office asked me to stop over after work, suddenly I came alive again. It was risky, dangerous sex; that's all it was, for her and for me, but it sure beat the blasé relationship I had at home."

Any relationship tends to become stagnant if not constantly infused with the fresh oils of love. At some point in most marriages, the partners can relate to Lewis Grizzard's book title, *If Love Were Oil, I'd Be About a Quart Low.*

Of course, passion cools with time. Nothing remains

static except static. Most of life around us is in a *deevolutionary* process; machines rust, cars wear out, beaches erode, the strongest of bridges and buildings need constant patching and repair simply to slow down the inevitable breaking apart. Yet, people such as Steve insist upon believing the myth that a good marriage will continue to perk right along with little or no refurbishing or realignment.

Even marvelous marriages, if not given proper attention, will lean toward monotony and boredom after a few years. Routines can become ruts, then ridges, creating mounting tension that can roadblock a relationship. The normal, nitty-gritty stresses and strains of life are just that—normal and nitty-gritty.

The problem comes whenever otherwise sane marriage partners slip into a pattern of comparing normal and nitty-gritty to the supposed intrigue, excitement, and adventure of an extramarital affair. It's like comparing a Public Broadcasting Service documentary to a James Bond movie. One is real life; the other is a flight into fantasy. One man told me, "My marriage was like a 'MacNeil/Lehrer Report'; my affair was 'The Wide World of Sports,' complete with the thrill of victory and the agony of defeat."

A forty-year-old pastor's wife confessed, "My affair had everything—the tease, the chase, the catch, the exploding passion—all the elements that were missing from my marriage."

If you add a stiff dose of depression to loneliness, monotony, and boredom, the odds increase dramatically that you will be tempted by an affair. The lure of excitement appeals as the cure for your lack of fulfillment, and before you know it, you are looking for someone else to provide the stimulation you feel you need and deserve.

Let me warn you: it won't work. In fact, it is a vicious, self-perpetuating cycle: you are lonely because you are bored by your dull, monotonous routine; you feel as though life is passing you by. Therefore, you become depressed and try to escape your depression through an adulterous relationship. In most cases, the affair creates a sense of guilt and usually ends on a negative note, often with more hurt and bitterness, which leads to more loneliness and depression.

Affairs stemming from loneliness, boredom, monotony, or depression are especially foolish and destructive. They are also preventable. Understand, only two people can bring joy into your life: Jesus Christ and you. If you depend upon friends, family, or even your spouse to meet your deepest needs and make you happy, you will always be on the verge of a breakdown or a burnout. Only Jesus can satisfy your soul, and only you can choose His joy for your life.

4. *Rationalization of anger, or revenge, stemming from unresolved conflicts in the marriage.* This often is described as the "retaliatory affair." Christian men and women who would not think of committing adultery under other circumstances have succumbed to this temptation, and sometimes even sought it out, when anger, bitterness, and resentment have taken root. Frequently, this sort of affair is a form of revenge for some past fracture in the marriage. Sometimes it is a marriage partner's last-ditch effort to warn his or her spouse of an impending disaster in their relationship if they don't deal with some unresolved conflict. For Sharon, it was both.

Sharon admitted, "I wanted my affair to kick him where it hurts and keep on kicking." She continued bitterly, "Curt hurt me deeply back in our second year of marriage, and I've never quite gotten over it. I don't think I ever will, but at least now I feel I have gotten even."

The unfaithful partner need not reveal the existence of the affair in order to have his or her sense of revenge satisfied. Terry retaliated against Gwen's indifference to his work by getting involved in an adulterous relationship:

> Gwen didn't care about an area of my life that meant the world to me. All she could see was that it took me away from her more than the average job. On repeated occasions, we argued about my career, and I tried to make her understand how important it was to me, but she just wouldn't see it. She ridiculed my job and told me I was a fool for wasting my time there. Finally, I gave up trying to convince her otherwise.

> I quit my job and took a higher-paying but less satisfying position with a stable company. Gwen and I rarely argued anymore, and to all outward observers, it appeared as though we were happy. Maybe Gwen was, but I sure wasn't.

> I shared my feelings with a woman I had dated before getting married, and she felt sorry for me. She understood how much that career had meant to me, and she couldn't believe Gwen could be so callous. I don't know if she was doing it purposely or not, but she was saying all the right things. We went to bed together that night.

> She wasn't as pretty as Gwen, and in many ways, not nearly as suited for me as Gwen, but our affair went on for over two years. It only ended when I got transferred because of my new job. Every time I was in bed with my lover, I thought, "Boy, would this just kill

Gwen if she ever found out, but it serves her right."
A few times, I thought of telling Gwen about the affair myself, but I never have. I'm satisfied simply knowing that I have pulled this over on her.

Often the unfaithful partner rationalizes this type of affair in this manner: "I deserve better than what life [a spouse] has dealt me. I'm not doing anything any worse than what he [she] has already done to me. Therefore, even though I know it is wrong, under my circumstances, it must be okay to deceive my mate." Revenge is a particularly powerful form of "punishment" for a wrong suffered, but it can never solve a marriage problem and ultimately it is always destructive to the relationship.

5. *A warped "spiritualization" of the retaliatory affair.* It sounds like this: "I married the wrong person, so God understands my having this affair." Yes, God understands, but He still calls it sin, and the Bible makes it clear that God hates sin!

Gina told me:

I knew Greg had a drinking problem before we ever got married. He came to our wedding half soused. Before we married, Greg went to church with me and claimed to be a Christian, so I figured after we were married, things would change. They did—for the worse.

Three months into our marriage, Greg began staying out late with his buddies. He'd stagger in at midnight, stoned out of his mind. Often, a friend would have to drive him home and help me put him to bed.

One of his buddies who helped a lot was Bobby. Greg and Bobby were lifelong friends, but Bobby refused to drink. His dad had died an alcoholic, and Bobby had become a Christian at his father's funeral. He'd still go out with the guys, but he'd always be the "designated driver."

Night after night, Bobby helped me drag Greg up the stairs and flop him onto our bed. Then Bobby and I would sit in the living room and talk. He had big, strong shoulders, and I shed quite a few tears on them. One night, as Bobby was consoling me, he gently put his arm around me and kissed me. At first I recoiled in horror, but then I melted into his arms. We made love on the living room floor while Greg slept off a drunken stupor upstairs in the bedroom.

Bobby was the best man at our wedding, in every sense of the word. I should have married him instead of Greg. Our affair is still going on, and I don't want it to stop. Even though I know it is a sin, I feel that God understands. He knows Bobby and I share something special. Maybe if Greg ever straightens up, I could be a faithful wife to him, but until he does, I'm going to hang on to Bobby.

I talked with Gina for over an hour, reminding her of her marriage vows and her commitment to Christ. Nevertheless, she refused to give up her relationship with a man who was "there," for a relationship with Jesus Christ, who seemed "far away." In a sense, she blamed God for the entire mess. Her logic was, "God gave me Greg and our marriage didn't work out, so it's God's fault I've gotten into this affair. In fact, it might even be His will."

Ludicrous logic? Of course, yet I've heard similar rationalizations from scores of Christian men and women who are looking for a loophole in the Bible that will allow for their adultery. They are wasting their time; they won't find it because it is not there.

6. *Failure to meet each other's needs.* When your needs are not being met, you are vulnerable to an affair. Similarly, when your mate's needs are going unmet, he or she is a sitting duck for seduction.

In his informative book *His Needs, Her Needs* (Revell, 1986), Dr. Willard F. Harley, Jr., categorizes ten basic needs a husband and wife must have met in order to affair-proof their marriage.

His needs include:
1. Sexual fulfillment
2. Recreational companionship
3. An attractive spouse
4. Domestic support
5. Admiration

Her needs include:
1. Affection
2. Conversation
3. Honesty and openness
4. Financial support
5. Family commitment

Certainly, most husbands and wives desire to have *all* of these needs met, but it is the order of importance that is interesting.

A Husband's Hit List

1. *Sexual fulfillment.* Not surprisingly, Dr. Harley lists sex at the top of the heap for most men. When this need

is not met in marriage, a man may feel cheated and eventually look elsewhere for sexual satisfaction. Dr. Harley explains:

> When a man chooses a wife, he promises to remain faithful to her for life. This means that he believes his wife will be his only sexual partner "until death do us part." He makes this commitment because he trusts her to be as sexually interested in him as he is in her. He trusts her to be sexually available to him whenever he needs to make love and to meet all his sexual needs, just as she trusts him to meet her marital needs.
>
> Unfortunately, in many marriages the man finds that putting his trust in this woman has turned into one of the biggest mistakes of his life. He has agreed to limit his sexual experience to a wife who is unwilling to meet that vital need. He finds himself up the proverbial creek without a paddle. If his religious or moral convictions are strong, he may try to make the best of it. Some husbands tough it out, but many cannot. They find sex elsewhere.
>
> The unfaithful man justifies it in terms of his wife's failure to keep her sexual commitment to him. When she discovers his unfaithfulness, she may try to "correct her error" and improve their sexual relationship, but by then it is too late. She feels hurt and resentful, and he has become deeply involved in an affair.

2. *Recreational companionship.* By this, Dr. Harley means spending "playtime" together as a couple. In other words, "The couple that plays together, stays together."

Harley's contention is that most husbands really do want to enjoy recreational activities with their wives, rather than with "the guys." Honest. The trick to this is to determine which activities are mutually enjoyable. Any recreational activity that demeans, exhausts, or has a negative impact upon one or both of you should be abandoned.

3. *An attractive spouse.* A wife's physical appearance matters to her husband. It is not unimportant or irrelevant, as some modern, radical feminists would lead you to believe. He may have married you for your brains, wit, charm, personality, or your bucks, but believe it, your body did not go unnoticed. Your husband might even say, "Dear, I know you are four hundred pounds overweight, but you are still beautiful to me," and he may be telling the truth! But deep inside, every husband desires his wife to be physically attractive.

Understand, this does not mean a wife needs to look like a Hollywood movie star or the latest teenage rock 'n' roll queen. It does mean a wise wife who wants to help her husband remain faithful for life will attempt to maintain her physical features in a manner somewhat similar to the woman he married. Granted, aging takes its toll, but there is no excuse for a wife to allow her weight to balloon, to dress in a sloppy, repulsive manner, or to ignore simple hygiene and health and beauty aids. To do so is tantamount to presenting your husband with an all-expense-paid ticket to an affair.

Two friends of mine fit the stereotypical mold. Although Valerie was an attractive woman when she and Gary married, after two children, she has "let herself go." She uses little makeup, rarely combs her hair in a style that Gary finds attractive, and dresses in frumpy, floppy fashions from the fifties.

When Gary leaves for work each morning, the image he takes with him is that of a woman dressed in bedraggled nightclothes covered by a pink flannel robe, with over-stuffed fuzzy slippers on her feet. When Gary arrives at work, his senses are bombarded by a bevy of beauties, neatly dressed, sweet-smelling fragrances emanating from their bodies, hair styled meticulously, and eager to please him. Gary is the supervisor in a TV production company office.

Although he struggles to take his Christianity to work, Gary confessed to me that he has engaged in adulterous affairs with several women in his company and is currently seeing a scriptwriter. Gary loves Valerie, but he is ashamed of her appearance and does not find her physically attractive. Consequently, he lives with her but is having sex with someone else.

Certainly, a husband needs to give attention to his physical appearance, as well. Wives, however, tend to develop a tremendous tolerance for their husbands' physical features. A man may be bald and bulging but still be considered attractive and desirable by his wife. Women have a remarkable ability to look beyond appearance and love the person, even after the body has turned to mush. Most men are not so benevolent. Furthermore, while male physical attractiveness may be a factor in female infidelity, few wives get involved in extramarital affairs solely because of their husband's inattention to physical appearance.

A woman who wants to meet her husband's needs and help him avoid adultery should make an honest appraisal of her appearance and ask the question, "Am I looking my best for my husband?"

4. *Domestic support.* In other words, he needs his wife to help maintain peace, quiet, and order at home. While modern men may not expect as much as their forefathers in this area, most men still expect their wives to transform the house into a home. If a man works in a noisy, frenzied, chaotic, or high-pressure, treadmill-type environment, he hopes to return home at the end of a hard day's work to an island of tranquillity. If he consistently finds the opposite, he may seek solace somewhere else.

5. *Admiration.* Specifically, most husbands want to be admired by their wives. A husband may not mind being the low man on the totem pole at work, or he may not be shaken or surprised when the women don't whistle at him when he walks by on the beach, if he knows his wife believes he is Mr. Wonderful. As a wife, you need to understand that your husband is addicted to your admiration; he can hardly function without it. If he doesn't receive it from you, chances are extremely high that he will be tempted to find it in an adulterous relationship.

On the other hand, evidence abounds of the positive power of honest, uplifting praise. Oh? You want proof? Next time your husband wears a new cologne (warning: you may have to buy it for him), enthusiastically compliment him on how manly it makes him smell, or how sexually desirable it causes you to feel toward him. Then, watch out. He'll probably take a bath in the stuff!

Admiration is a marvelous motivator for most men. Dr. Harley comments:

> When a woman tells a man she thinks he's wonderful, that inspires him to achieve more. He sees himself as

capable of handling new responsibilities and perfecting skills far above those of his present level. . . . When she tells him that she appreciates him for what he has done, it gives him more satisfaction than he receives from his paycheck. A woman needs to appreciate her husband for what he already is, not for what he could become, if he lived up to her standards.

The doctor's observation is a practical application of this biblical principle: "Let the wife see to it that she respect her husband" (Ephesians 5:33). Consider this: The Bible does not specifically command a wife to *love* her husband, but it does demand that she *respect* her mate, whether he is worthy of that respect or not!

Just how desperately husbands depend upon their wives' respect and admiration is revealed by what inevitably happens when they do not receive it. Even men of strong moral fiber are tempted to be unfaithful. Some men sublimate their need for admiration by pouring themselves into their work, sports, or a hobby. Others seek consolation at the local watering hole where, after a few drinks, they begin boasting of exploits that never happened, except in their dreams. To most husbands, nothing can adequately compensate for the lack of a wife's admiration.

Certainly, not all men yield to temptation, but many do. Frequently, when the affair is discovered, people wag their heads (and their tongues) and say, "What did he ever see in her?" Often, it wasn't what he saw; it was an unmet need for admiration that opened the door to adultery.

Barb and Mark are an affair in the making. They have been happily married for sixteen years and have three beautiful children. He is a highly motivated, energetic, successful salesman and she is a vivacious, active mother and homemaker. Their love for each other is unquestionable.

So what's the problem? Barb is a whiner; she is constantly on Mark's case about something, nitpicking, criticizing, and complaining. Although he bends over backward to please her, whatever he does is not quite good enough. Rarely does Barb compliment or give Mark credit for his accomplishments. Instead, she incessantly harps about any minor foibles or failures he might exhibit. She frequently makes fun of him in front of their friends and even speaks sarcastically about Mark to his mother.

Mark is not a bozo. He is a dedicated Christian husband and father; he is talented, good-looking, and has a lot going for him. Unfortunately, Barb's self-image is so fragile and insecure that she feels by praising Mark she would be deprecating herself.

Barb may not realize it, but her husband is starving for her admiration and respect. If he doesn't get it from her, sooner or later, he is going to seek it from someone else. Despite his commitment to Christ, to his wife, and to his children, all it will take to trigger temptation is for some sweet, young thing to say, "Oh, Mark! You're so strong," or "Mark, you are *so* talented," or some similar compliment, and Mark's defenses will fall faster than the walls of Jericho.

Forgive me if I sound fatalistic or fanatical about this cause for affairs, but I have seen too many fine husbands and fathers done in due to "admiration deficiency."

Most married men—especially Christian married men—do not cheat on their wives simply to have sex. A husband's knowledge of biblical injunctions condemning adultery or his own spiritual and moral strength may cause him to tolerate a less-than-satisfying sexual relationship with his wife. But if his wife refuses to respect him, a husband is psychologically (and perhaps spiritually) emasculated. Any wife who does not let her husband know she appreciates and admires him should not be surprised when she catches him in somebody else's bed.

What Are Her Needs?

1. *Affection*. While sex may rank number one on most husbands' lists, many men are surprised to discover that their wives prefer affection to the physical act of intercourse. Husband: It is virtually impossible to give your wife too much affection. She thrives on it; some days she *survives* on your tender expressions of love. Nothing else will do.

You need to *tell* your wife you love her. Don't assume that because you told her once, long ago, it still counts. One old codger complained, "Tell her I love her? I married her, didn't I? Isn't that enough?"

Nope. She needs to hear those three magic words (no, not "Let's eat out"). I'm talking about *I love you*. Let's practice now, guys. Open wide. "I." "La, la, love." "Ya, ya, ya (pretend you are cheering for your favorite football team), you!" See, I knew you could do it. Now, keep practicing and when she least expects it, lay an "I love you" on her. Hold her close and look right into her eyes as you say it. Be sure to watch her eyes carefully so you can tell when she regains consciousness.

Beyond expressing your love in words, husband, you need to *show* your wife you love her. She needs those affectionate touches, caresses, and glances. She needs you to express your love in ways that don't always lead to the bedroom. How long has it been since you brought home a two-dollar rose for your wife? Of course, a two-dollar rose costs five bucks nowadays, but it's the thought that counts, right? When was the last time you took your wife out to dinner, just the two of you? Can't afford it? Okay. How about a picnic or a walk in the park? Do something, *anything*, that shows her she is special to you.

Myrtle, a sweet, sex-starved saint, was shocked to hear her pastor reveal in a sermon that when he wanted to show his wife how much he loved her, he nibbled on her ear. Myrtle was intrigued by the idea.

When she arrived home from church, Herman, her husband, was propped in front of the television set, watching a baseball game.

"Herman?" Myrtle cooed.

"Yes, Myrtle."

"Herman, Pastor Smith said that whenever he feels romantic and wants to let his wife know how much he loves her, he nibbles on her ear."

"Yeah, right. So what, Myrtle?"

"Herman . . . why don't you ever nibble on *my* ear?"

"Why don't I what? Myrtle, that's ridiculous! Now, go sit down. Can't you see I'm watching the ball game?"

"Herman . . . Pastor nibbles on his wife's ear. . . ."

"Myrtle, it's the last inning of the World Series. Won't you please get out of the way?"

"Herman—why won't you nibble on my ear?"

"Oh, all right, Myrtle! I'll nibble on your ear. Go out to the refrigerator and get my false teeth!"

Affection. No wife wants to live without it.

2. *Conversation.* Dr. Harley counsels married men to give their mates a *minimum* of fifteen hours a week for undivided attention and communication. When husbands balk, Harley says, "I don't bat an eye, but simply ask them how much time they spent giving their wives undivided attention during their courting days. Any bachelor who fails to devote something close to fifteen hours a week to his girl friend faces the strong likelihood of losing her."

Many a husband has lost his wife to an extramarital affair simply because he couldn't or wouldn't find the time to communicate with her.

Most marriage counselors can't even estimate how many times they have heard the complaint, "We just don't talk anymore." A husband's failure to communicate is a leading factor in female infidelity.

Debbie is typical of many devoted wives who defect for an affair. She said sorrowfully:

> Fred simply quit talking to me, so I finally went out and found somebody who would. At first, I wasn't looking for an affair. I just needed some meaningful conversation. I met Bruce at my son's elementary school play. He asked me about my opinions on literature, art, music, and a host of other things. It really caught me off guard. I wasn't accustomed to somebody really wanting to hear my ideas. First we had lunch, then one thing led to another.

Husband: Your wife *needs* you to talk with her, and not merely about mundane tripe. She wants to know what you are thinking and feeling, and she wants you to ask about her opinions and ideas, as well. Conversation to her means more than a faceless "uh-huh" from behind a newspaper. And she does not want to compete with the television while she talks with you. Your wife wants, needs, and deserves your undivided attention. If you don't give it to her, somebody else will.

3. *Honesty and openness.* These rank high on Dr. Harley's list of a wife's needs. Bluntly, a wife must be able to trust her husband, and a smart husband will give her every reason to do so. Anything that destroys confidence in your faithfulness should be avoided at all costs. It's just not worth it.

Early in my dating relationship with Angela, I learned this lesson the hard way. On my way back from Michigan to Pennsylvania, following a fabulous visit with Angela and her family, I stopped to visit some mutual friends. One member of the family with whom I visited was a young woman Angela regarded with no small amount of suspicion. My brief stay was innocuous and uneventful, but when Angela found out about it, she was angry and hurt.

I realized the pain I had caused my future wife, and I determined then and there to remove or avoid any cause for questioning and doubt concerning my actions or motives. To do otherwise would be foolish.

4. *Financial support.* By this, Dr. Harley means that a wife and mother needs to know the family's basic financial needs are going to be met. Constant scrimping and scraping to make ends meet will grate on any marriage relationship.

Jackie left her husband, Michael, taking with her their four children, all under eight years of age. She confided:

When I thought about leaving, it was frightening, but I just couldn't take it anymore. I was willing to do almost anything to help Michael in his career, but he'd spend money as if we were rolling in it. Meanwhile, I barely had enough change to buy food for the kids' breakfasts. It was a constant hassle for us. We had to wear two and three sweaters in the winter because we couldn't afford to pay our heating oil bill. Our windows had frost on the inside. When the electric company turned off the power because we hadn't paid our bills, and I knew Michael had gotten paid that week, I said, "That's it. I'm out of here." I left.

Jackie moved in with Michael's best friend, Artie. It wasn't lack of money that caused the affair; it was lack of security.

5. *Family commitment.* Every wife needs to know that after God, she and her children come first in her husband's life. That sounds simple enough, but being a good husband is a tough chore; to be an excellent father, as well, requires supernatural doses of unconditional and sacrificial love. Only the Lord can supply that sort of strength.

My friend Tim Hansel is a talented author, speaker, and ministry executive, but whenever someone asks Tim what he does, he wells up with pride and answers, "I'm a dad!" That's the kind of commitment most wives long for from their husbands.

What are some things a husband can do to show his commitment to the family? Attend birthday parties, school events, and church services. He can read to the kids before bedtime, help with homework, plan family outings and vacations, and perhaps most important, eat as many meals as possible at home with the troops. There's just something about Dad sitting at the head of the table that instills confidence in the children and loving security in a wife.

Harley's hints hold out hope for a "heavenly" marriage, but they also present a serious warning:

> Whenever a wife finds a husband who exhibits all five qualities, she will find him irresistible. But a note of caution: If he exhibits only four of them, she will experience a void that will nag persistently and incessantly for fulfillment. . . .
>
> When a man finds a woman who exhibits all five qualities, he will find her irresistible. But again the same note of caution must be sounded for the woman that sounded for the man. If a wife meets only four of her husband's five basic needs, he will experience a void that can lead to problems.

Ironically, it takes much more effort for you to keep your partner faithful than it does for a false lover to lure your mate toward infidelity. That is the powerful attraction of adultery: somebody else will meet the need or needs that are not being met in your marriage. It is also the awful lie. For example, you may be meeting eight of your spouse's basic ten needs, but in those two deficient areas, you can be certain the door is open to adultery.

Should someone come along who seems willing to meet those two needs, the temptation is to ignore the other eight areas of satisfaction and chase after the person who can satisfy the two. Often, the unfaithful partner soon discovers that the false lover can *only* meet those two needs. Now, instead of having eight of ten needs met, only two are being satisfied, which may account for why a person who divorces to marry his or her lover often ends up in another divorce.

The message here is twofold: First, you must seek to satisfy all ten needs; second, if all of your needs are not currently being met, don't be deluded into jumping out of the frying pan into the fire of an affair. Thank God for what you have in your marriage, and begin working to make it better.

Is There Life After an Affair?

Most marriage counselors resoundingly agree: Yes! There is hope for a marriage that has suffered an affair. But it won't be easy, and a couple may never be quite the same. A precious commitment has been broken and it will take time, work, and unconditional love to repair it. A reason existed for the affair, and it must be rectified.

As in any traumatic experience, people respond with a raft of emotions. Anger. Denial. Self-righteousness. Hurt. Bitterness. Blame. Acquiescence. Revenge. Once an affair happens, it is a fact that must be faced. How a couple *chooses to feel* about that fact will determine whether their relationship will survive or sink under the load of excess baggage left by the affair. Many times, couples give up too easily.

J. Allan Petersen says in *The Myth of the Greener Grass*, "Many husbands and wives think it is easier to call it quits than to repair the marriage. When it's too late they find they took the easiest way out but not the wisest."

Forgiveness will be one of the most important factors in recovering from an affair. Remember, although only one of you may have been unfaithful to the marriage, both of you are at fault; both share some responsibility for the affair. Therefore, *both* you and your spouse should repent before God and apologize to each other.

Each of you should ask to receive forgiveness from the other, and each of you should *verbally* express the forgiveness that is granted. One of the toughest promises you may ever make will be this one: "I forgive you, and I will attempt to never mention this affair again—not to my family or friends, not even to myself. It is over and done."

It will also be necessary to extend forgiveness to the third party in an affair. Seek the Lord's wisdom as to whether this forgiveness should be expressed in person or merely by extending that forgiveness from your heart, releasing all anger, bitterness, and resentment in the process. In most cases, the latter is better. The Holy Spirit will guide you in this matter, and if a personal encounter is required, He will provide a private, discreet opportunity, perhaps with a chance to minister emotional healing and spiritual restoration.

You must also forgive yourself. Whatever your role in the affair, once it is confessed to God and forgiveness is sought between the offending parties, you must forgive yourself. To do otherwise is to insult the Lord Jesus Christ, who sacrificed His life to pay the penalty for your sins. Once forgiveness takes place, you are ready to begin rebuilding your marriage. It won't be easy, but it can be done.

The Lord can heal your marriage, but first you must allow Him to heal your heart. Have faith; He can do it! Granted, even with God's healing balm, wounds from an affair will not disappear overnight. But be encouraged. As

Dr. Kinder and Dr. Cowan observe in *Husbands and Wives*, "Healing typically takes more time than one hopes, but less time than one fears."

How to Avoid an Affair

Here are eight suggestions for fending off infidelity in your marriage (you'll notice we have elaborated upon each of these points in the last two chapters):

1. Give your spouse top priority in your life, second only to God.
2. Lavish compliments upon your mate. Build up, rather than tear down, your partner's self-esteem.
3. Communicate rather than complain.
4. Focus upon the positive aspects of your marriage.
5. Make sex and romance a never-ending priority in your relationship.
6. Constantly seek to meet each other's needs.
7. Be willing to change.
8. Never take your partner for granted.

Remember, the idea that an affair could never happen to you is a myth. But by trusting Jesus Christ as the Foundation for your marriage, and by paying heed to the principles within this chapter, an affair need never happen to you. You can build a lifelong, fulfilling marriage relationship.

11
The Bubbles Have Burst

Marriage Myth Number Ten:
You can't revive what isn't alive. Or, "Can we really build a future together?"

"It's true that love is blind, but marriage is sure an eye-opener!"

Mary Anne Rogers

● ● ● ● ● ● ● ● ● ● ● ● ●

My kitchen sink faucet is dripping . . . and dripping . . . and dripping. I wouldn't mind, but Angela, Ashleigh, and I just spent our life savings to move out of our tiny apartment—an apartment with a pesky, perpetually leaking kitchen sink faucet—into a lovely, spacious new house we had built especially for us. What a surprise it was to discover that our new house came complete with a leaking faucet . . . just to make us feel at home, I guess.

Building a house is an exasperating experience. So many details to decide, so many opportunities to disagree; it's a wonder any couple survives the closing date.

Ah! But now that we are settled into our new home, all the frustration we endured, from building foremen, loan officers, lawyers, and landscapers to garbage removers, seems to have faded into the walls. We are blissfully happy, bounding from one room to another, opening boxes that took weeks to pack.

As with any new house, ours has a few rough spots that need to be worked out and touched up by the builder. I found three cans of paint in the cabinet beneath our sink; I think that's a hint.

Maybe I should be angry over my leaking kitchen sink faucet, but I'm not. It goes with the territory, a minor irritation amid a major improvement in our lives. Oh, sure; the builder could have done it perfectly the first time. Any plumber worth his pipes knows how to install a kitchen sink faucet. No doubt, he'll get it right sooner or later . . . because I'm going to continue calling that contractor until he does.

I admit, there were times during the building process when Angela and I were ready to throw in the towel, tear up the contract, and forget it. We could have done so legally and morally. We had plenty of just cause. The contractor constructing our house knew it, the bank knew it, and so did we. But we stuck to our commitment and worked through the many problems, setbacks, mistakes, and disappointments. Now, as we relax in our new home, we are quick to say it was worth all the hassles.

If I could just get that faucet to quit dripping. . . .

The Importance of Hanging in There

Building a great marriage is similar to building a house—only tougher. At times you will be frustrated, exasperated, and tempted to give up on the whole deal. You'll feel like reneging on your original commitment and going to Hawaii to be a beach bum (at least, that's where I'd go).

Don't do it! Hang in there. Keep working; keep growing; keep building, even if your marriage requires a major remodeling job. But don't demolish the entire house simply because you have a leaking faucet.

Sadly, when the sugar-sweet myths of marriage turn sour, some marriage partners will do almost anything to get away from each other, regardless of the cost. Other couples lapse into "peaceful coexistence," living in the same house but not building a life together.

One fellow in his mid-forties put it this way: "Our marriage died a slow death many years ago. It's too late for us now. You can't revive what isn't alive."

Not true! Our God specializes in bringing the dead back to life. Remember Lazarus (John 11)? Elijah and the widow's son (1 Kings 17)? Elisha and the Shunammite woman's little boy (2 Kings 4)? Jairus' daughter (Mark 5)? What about Jesus Himself (Luke 24)? What do they have in common? They were all dead, but the power of God brought them back to life.

Furthermore, the Bible reveals that the same power that raised Christ Jesus from the dead is available to deliver you from the doldrums, devastation, and despair of sin and to raise you up to a new life-style on earth as well as to provide you with the promise of eternal existence in heaven. The Apostle Paul explained this miracle to the Christians at Ephesus:

> And you were dead in your trespasses and sins, in which you formerly walked according to the course of this world. . . .
>
> But God, being rich in mercy, because of His great love with which He loved us, even when we were

dead in our transgressions, made us alive together
with Christ (by grace you have been saved), and
raised us up with Him, and seated us with Him in the
heavenly places, in Christ Jesus, in order that in the
ages to come He might show the surpassing riches of
His grace in kindness toward us in Christ Jesus.

Ephesians 2:1–7

If we take Paul's words seriously, there no longer remains an excuse for living trivial, lackluster lives; Jesus offers much more than mere peaceful coexistence. He offers
resurrection *power*, resurrection *love*, resurrection *life*. As
my friend Mike Warnke often says, "Jesus didn't come to
make bad people good; He came to make dead people live!"

The Lord can do that in your marriage as well as in your
personal life, if you will give Him the opportunity. Start by
establishing your "house" upon the solid Rock, Jesus
Christ. Trust Him as the foundation for your life and marriage. Then begin building slowly and carefully according
to His blueprint, the Bible. When all else fails, read the
directions!

It won't be easy. Even a new house, built upon a firm
foundation, requires constant upkeep. Remember? *Marriage takes work.*

In Every Marriage, There's a Bit of Manure

As I write these words, I can look out my study window
into the backyard. It's covered with straw and manure
right now—a real mess. If Angela, Ashleigh, and I hope to
frolic upon a lush, green lawn next summer, I'll have to
work all through the spring to get the grass to grow. It will

be costly, demanding, tiring, and time-consuming. A healthy yard requires fertilizing, watering, and reseeding, not to mention dealing with the clumps of dung the landscaper left behind. Nevertheless, after nursing my lawn to life, working feverishly, and anointing it often, along with the laying on of hands and begging God to allow a few blades of grass to grow, I'll probably still mumble, grumble, and complain whenever it's time to mow the lawn. That's life.

Maintaining and improving this property will be work; there will be bills to pay and sacrifices to make, but I'll love it—except for the one day each month when I write the check for our house payment!

When building a house or building a marriage, you must count the costs, unmask the myths, burst the bubbles, and face reality. Hiding your eyes from the truth can be extremely dangerous. A town in Kentucky passed a law making it illegal for anyone over the age of twelve to wear a mask in public. If only we could pass a law like that for marriage partners!

Don't be afraid to remove the masks. Always remember this: God is not turned off by what you are; He knows what you are . . . and still loves you! That truth in itself is astounding, but perhaps the greater miracle is that He provides the same sort of unconditional, sacrificial, indefatigable love for all who will depend upon Him. His perfect love can empower you and your marriage partner to unmask the myths of marriage, yet love each other more deeply than either of you ever dreamed possible. That is the miracle of His supernatural, superabounding love at work in and through you!

At Angela's and my wedding, my brother sang a song

he and I had written especially for the occasion. The lyrics are based upon the Apostle Paul's grand definition of true love found in 1 Corinthians 13:

> Everybody's talking about love these days,
> But I think we've gotten confused.
> Love's not something you can do for me;
> Love is what I give to you.
>
> I told you that I love you
> And you know I'll always be true.
> My love for you will always remain,
> No matter what you do.
>
> True love is patient;
> True love is kind;
> Love is not jealous when I just need some time.
> Real love bears all things;
> True love believes all things.
> True love endures all things;
> Hopes all things,
> But true love never fails!
>
> So when you get tired at the end of the day,
> Maybe feelin' a little bit blue;
> Come on home to where you know you belong;
> You'll find a love that's true.
>
> 'Cause true love is patient;
> True love is kind;
> Love is not jealous when I just need some time.
> Real love bears all things;
> True love believes all things.
> True love endures all things;
> Hopes all things,
> But true love never fails!

That marvelous, miraculous kind of love is possible in your marriage as you and your partner come together, with Jesus Christ in the center of your relationship. It is yours for the asking.

A young couple has purchased the tract of land next to ours and has begun the process of building a house. I suppose I'd better pray for them—they're going to need it. Each day, another truckload of materials arrives and a small army of construction workers voraciously consumes the supplies as they race to complete the house before the closing date. Soon, our new neighbors will be moving into their new home, excited about beginning a fresh life together.

Hmmm, I wonder if one of them knows how to fix a leaking faucet. . . .